ELEMENTAL
Alejandro Aravena

LOUISIANA MUSEUM OF MODERN ART
LARS MÜLLER PUBLISHERS

Supported by Realdania
Sponsor of architectural exhibitions
at Louisiana Museum of Modern Art

ELEMENTAL
Alejandro Aravena

**Interview with Alejandro Aravena
by Michael Juul Holm**

Foreword

When the Louisiana Museum of Modern Art mounts an architecture exhibition, it usually also involves a wish to open a window into the architect's work process: How does the architect do it? What does he or she think prior to the form? How does architecture move from concept to design to construction, and what is the cultural impact?

The answers are numerous, of course, and more important, they come in very different types. Talking process with the Chilean studio Elemental, no particular theory or pre-determined vocabulary of forms is advanced as an explanation for a finished building. Instead, the human body and sensation play crucial roles. Elemental's method is to start from scratch every time and put everything that occurs to them into play – thoughts, meetings, conversations – before finally trimming all the fat. That is the architectural process here. If the forms of their buildings seem basic, the process leading to them is anything but.

The architect's process is what we are after in our exhibition series *The Architect's Studio*, which kicked off in 2016 with the Chinese architect Wang Shu. The second show in the series, *So Far... ELEMENTAL / Alejandro Aravena* looks at a new generation of architects who, in their own ways, are helping to redefine the architect's role. Process is the signature move of Elemental and its founder and frontman, Alejandro Aravena. Communicating the studio's projects – some still on the drawing board, others realized, from small design object to grand master plan – this publication puts a premium on reproducing Aravena's sketches and his studio's striking, raw models. Next, the selection of works was guided by Elemental's monolithic building projects, which display a near-Brutalist choice of materials and the studio's concern for primary – elemental – architectural forces. A separate section deals with Elemental's first realized project, the so-called Half a House, which put the studio on the map, with its pioneering and sustainable solution to an urgent problem in Chile's slums: How do you build sustainable housing on a tight budget, while providing a certain standard of living and making room for communal life between the buildings? Elemental's concept, with variations, can be used all over the world. True to the idea of open source design, the studio on its website posted a manual for building the Half a House, free for anyone to use. In Chile, they have built several variants of the house. The projects shown here are just a small part of the public housing projects that the studio has realized since the first one in 2011.

The exhibition's title, *So Far ...*, should be read as a retrospective look at the studio's output until now. Moreover, the title denotes the distance between Chile and Denmark, which may involve different worldviews but does not affect the human sense of space, weight, gravity, balance – the elemental things. While many architects and engineers push the envelope with spectacular shapes defying the laws of nature, Elemental strives for simple, almost obvious, common-sense forms.

In connection with the exhibition, Alejandro Aravena was interviewed for this catalogue. The interview falls into four sections that mark important basic approaches in Elemental's practice and philosophy. As a point of departure, the studio always strives to find out what questions the building should answer, instead of merely responding to the client's immediate wishes. What actual factors, needs, site-specific climate conditions and day-to-day routines make up the building's function, its future prospects and sustainability in all respects? People have a lot of dreams about buildings. The architect has the skills to convert

such dreams into the one question that will lead to the best design answer. Aravena discusses this in the chapter titled *Not the Answer but the Question: Looking at Constraints and Possibilities in Giving Form to the Built Environment.*

The chapter *Balance, Equilibrium and Sustainability* examines the fascination with inevitable natural forces, while the chapters *Being Good or Doing Good: Professionalism as a Tool* and *Open Source Creativity: Design as a Participatory Process* include discussions of the role of architects today, the altruistic perspective of Elemental's public housing projects and how the real issue should be the quality of the architect's work. User involvement is key to Elemental's practice, and the studio has developed its own user-involvement tool, Workshop Elemental. Elemental's designs always address real life. The studio is not just a think tank, it is also a 'do tank'.

Without the ongoing support of Realdania, including for *The Architect's Studio* series, a lot of things would be very different at the Louisiana. We hold to the belief that architecture exhibitions make a significant contribution to the growing awareness in society of our potential place in the world as humans, how we live together, our dreams and visions. Warm thanks to Realdania, to Michael Juul Holm for interviewing Alejandro Aravena and finally, of course, to Elemental and Alejandro Aravena.

Poul Erik Tøjner
Director, Louisiana Museum of Modern Art

Kjeld Kjeldsen
Curator

Mette Marie Kallehauge
Co-Curator

STAAB BOHM
ELEMENTAL

Far from Elementary

By Mette Marie Kallehauge

Regular forms and monolithic buildings made of raw, unprocessed materials with an almost Brutalist primitiveness: Elemental have not made their name in the world of contemporary architecture with spectacular structures and state-of-the-art materials, but rather by taking a step back and working with far more basic forces like gravity, the climate, and humankind. Which often makes their solutions so apt that we find ourselves thinking: of course! Of course – just one example – a building in Santiago should not be made of glass. The hot climate here demands a heavy thermal mass, not a greenhouse. The 'eureka' experience is intense. How do Elemental reach this kind of insight? By not having any preconceived ideas about form or narrative, and by taking an elementary approach.

The Chilean architects initially became famous for the social housing project they designed for a slum on the outskirts of the capital Santiago. Their controversial approach of designing 'half houses' so the people living in them could make the other half themselves was not only about creating a new type of dwelling, but about addressing the realities of life in the slum. Experience had shown that the people living in makeshift dwellings here always extended their homes to a minimum of 80 m² using their own limited funds and – sometimes – limited skills. So instead of building the 40 m² possible within the state budget, Elemental decided to create a framework for 80 m² with all the basic structures and installations that would make it easier and safer for people to extend their home themselves. This pragmatic yet revolutionary way of thinking is key to Elemental's architecture, where there is no single way to build or approach architecture, but as many as there are projects, clients, and contractors. Elemental do not approach projects with a specific style of architecture in mind – their trademark is process and method and the way they ask questions about the context of a building. As they themselves put it: "There is nothing worse than the right answer to the wrong question." Their mission is to identify the right question.

Process is everything: Workshop Elemental

There is a huge focus on branding architects and architectural projects today, to which communication is key. And the founder of Elemental,

Top: *The Value of What is not Built*. The contribution by Elemental to the Venice Architecture Biennale 2018, presenting seven hand-written statements on 'Open System Design'. Original sketches, hand-made models, and project images printed on A4, are folded and hung on strings pinned directly to the wall. Bottom: The office of Elemental, Autumn 2018.

Alejandro Aravena, is also a gifted communicator with a unique way of conveying ideas that has definitely contributed to Elemental's success. Aravena has been awarded the Pritzker Prize, the most prestigious in the world of architecture, and in 2016 he also curated the Venice Biennale of Architecture, the most important architecture exhibition in the world. It could be claimed that prestige is no longer solely about creating good architecture, but more about the stories told about it. But instead of telling stories about buildings, Elemental would much rather talk about the process at the core of their practice. Talking about the architecture itself is secondary to the experience of space, gravity, and materiality. So working on a solo exhibition it is not only about documenting their work, but also about how they approach making an exhibition, which in itself becomes an insight-generating investigation of the essence of architecture. This makes an exhibition no different to a piece of architecture for Elemental, and like their architecture the experience is more bodily and sensory than intellectual. The exhibition is thus not just illustrations or images: Elemental's documentation of every single step of the process is the extra layer that unveils their approach to architecture. In their world it is the detailed record and analysis of the process as it happens that creates the durability of the form as well as functionality of a building.

Part of this process is including as many different factors or 'parameters' in design development as possible. And it is perfectly fine if these different parameters pull the project in different directions. Opposing forces create the tension or synthesis necessary for the form to emerge. The parameters are what the architects say "inform the form of the project." If the assignment is to build a bank, then Elemental interview everyone from the security staff to the catering company that is going to provide the staff lunch about their work routines. Part of the building's sustainability is that in addition to the core services provided by the bank, all the invisible cogwheels that make it function fit perfectly in the engine that runs it. If the bank is located close to a slum that poses a threat to security, then 'slum', 'crime' and 'security' become parameters that generate a higher level of synthesis in the project. So instead of giving up in the face of such challenges by moving the bank to a safer area or building a security wall around it,

Working on the exhibition *So Far … ELEMENTAL | Alejandro Aravena* at Louisiana Museum of Modern Art. The installation of a 'floating cube' is taking form in sketches and cardboard models.

Elemental develop a 'total solution' that brings positive urban regeneration to the area by surrounding the bank with a new park raised to a level of 18 metres on a bridge that had to be built anyway. Again – of course! This kind of community inclusion is part of what the architects call WE – Workshop Elemental – and forms the framework of every new project.

Mathematics and Intuition

The use of mathematical concepts like equations and variables, plus the inclusion of so many different users' voices that inform the architecture, can make Elemental's process look complicated. But alongside the systematic chaos of Workshop Elemental lies a deep fascination with simple solutions, which are the goal of the complex synthesis. As in the laws of physics, equilibrium arises out of chaos. Elemental's architecture is created by working with simple forms and the fundamental forces of gravity and weight, forces so elementary that we rarely think about them. The simple, incontrovertible relationship between gravity and volume in nature characterises Elemental's work. We have all seen architecture that uses engineering to controvert the most fundamental laws of nature and make buildings do things we did not believe was possible, but this is not what Elemental do. Instead they try to point out things that are right in front of us but that we might not notice in our everyday lives: the simple yet powerful forces that are the very foundation of architecture. They point to the factual circumstances of a project and say: "Look, it's that simple." Elemental's is the art of transforming facts into form.

As they put it themselves, some forces are simply "larger than life." The laws of mathematics and physics are incontrovertible, and can be used in their simplest form to steer the architecture. Such laws are tools for Elemental, as is their intuition. They often mention intuition as a powerful element in creating a project: the kind of intuition involved when the architect meets the client, when one person meets another, when some things are said and others unsaid, the way people speak, a specific gesture. This atmosphere and energy bring an element of chance to the process. Creating buildings that could last for centuries based on intuition is liberating. But most liberating of

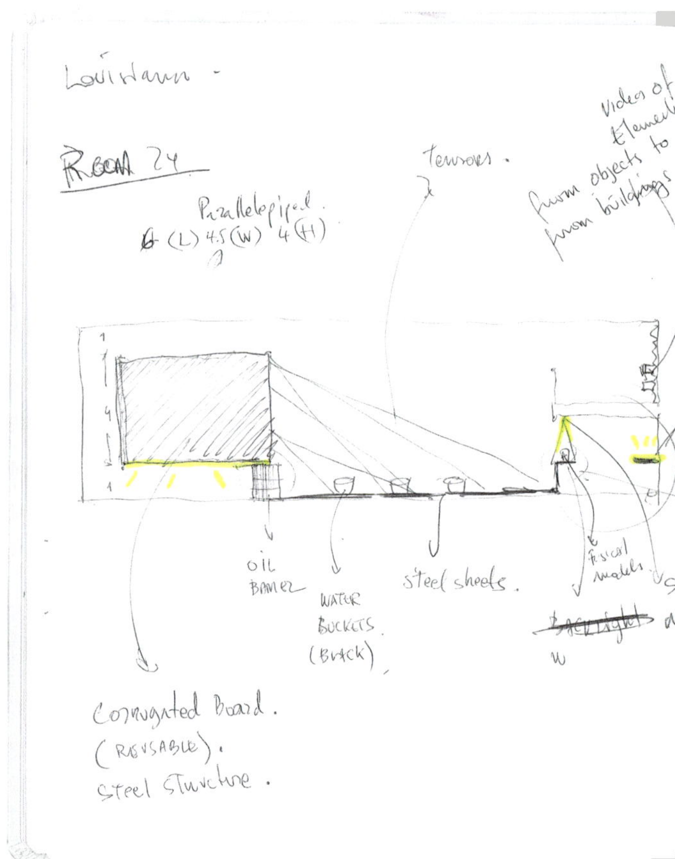

all it is that this is not what Elemental use to 'sell' their projects. Intuition is always counterbalanced by common sense. We are not dealing with the 'divine inspiration' of a master artist: the intuition central to Elemental's work always corresponds to an invariable, like the force of gravity or budget. Many architects would probably describe their work in the same way, but for Elemental it is key: hard-core project parameters and intuition are of equal professional value in the end equation of form.

The common sense of sustainability

Elemental's investigation of the elementary, of basic conditions given form through design, sharpens their own understanding of design. This is the kind of investigation that lies behind the design of their Chairless Chair. The project started with a simple question: What does it mean to sit? What does the body do? How do we rest our legs? How did people first sit comfortably on the ground? Elemental often return to primal behaviour, transforming their questions and investigations into statements or projects that determine the direction the architecture takes. These investigations can also tell us something about sustainability. Because sustainability does not have to be limited to 'green' buildings, recycling, or CO2 consumption. It can also be about simplifying things as a way to detox from the consumer world we live in, which depletes our minds and bodies as much as the planet we live on.

Chairless Chair is a good example of Elemental's approach to sustainability. The chair is simply a strap that makes it possible to sit on the ground as we would do naturally, but in a more comfortable way where the hands and arms are free, maybe to hold a book or tablet. The project – a small experiment – is based on the fundamental idea that pervades all Elemental's projects, from small design objects to large buildings, where everything superfluous is stripped away, and where sustainability is also an issue of simplified form and structure. This penchant for the primitive can also be seen in the way Elemental present their projects. Computer-generated renderings are rare. They prefer raw yet beautiful wooden models that make the architecture highly present to the senses and manifest their

Selecting 120 sketchbooks with original sketches at the office of Elemental in Santiago for the exhibition *So Far ... ELEMENTAL | Alejandro Aravena*. The books are meant to lie on a counterweight installation made entirely of cardboard.

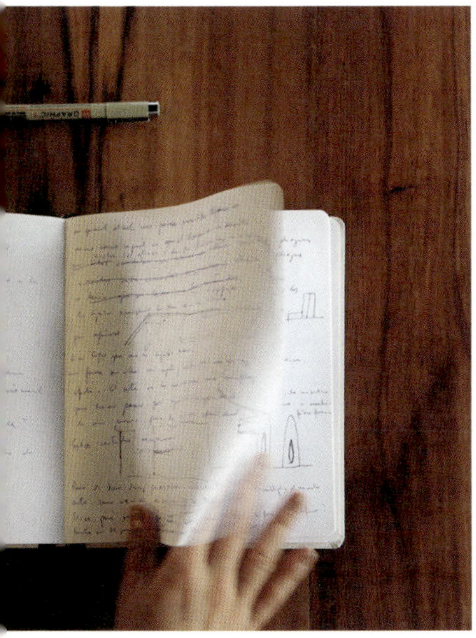

principles of simplicity and making do with what you have. From the presentation of the project to the completed building, integrity prevails.

Elemental's sustainable projects have won numerous awards, including the Swedish Gothenburg Sustainability Award (2017), the first prize of the Austrian Zumtobel Group Award Urban Developments & Initiatives (2014), the American World Green Building Council Chairman's Award (2014), and the Danish Index Award (2011). Even though their practice is entirely sustainable, they do not operate with the concept of 'sustainability'. Elemental just call it common sense.

Elemental neither pose nor pretend. Their process is honest and straightforward, stringently structured using the tool of Workshop Elemental where chaos reigns until each and every parameter has been discussed and examined from every angle. The method is based on a special kind of conversation and a shared fascination with human invention. Plus a sense of solidarity that might be the reason the five partners have decided to stick to the twenty people they are now. That Elemental is a collective endeavour with a shared mindset is what makes their method possible. Natural curiosity and the discussion of new inventions, technology, human history and everyday life over lunch at the office are what fuel their work. This is where they find inspiration and talk through solutions. As Aravena says: "It is no more complicated, but also no more simple than that." In the same vein, we could maybe say that architecture might not be such an enigma, but is also no more elementary than it takes architects to create it.

Lookout Point Espinazo del Diablo Jalisco, Mexico

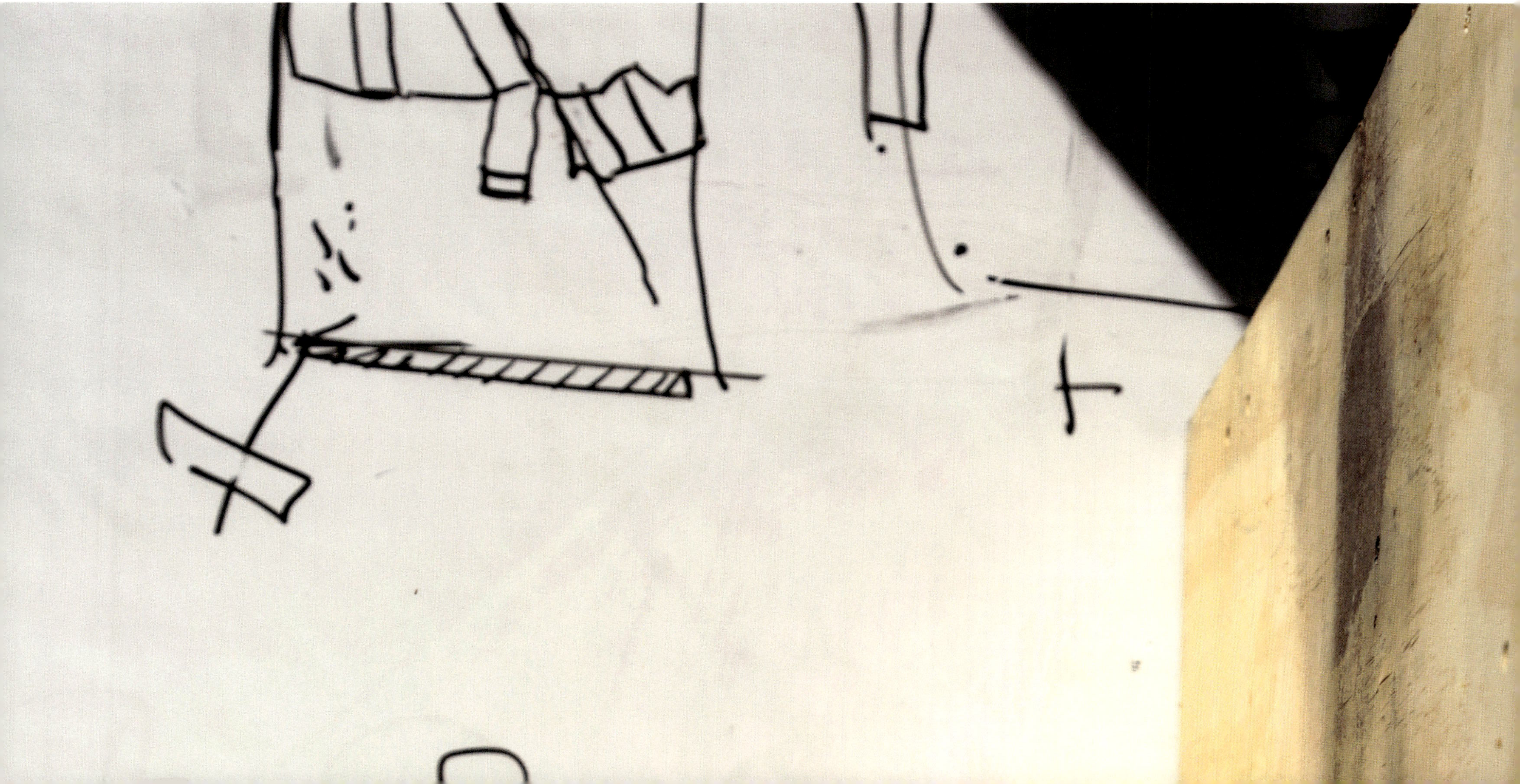

The lookout point is the highest point on the pilgrim route from Ameca to Talpa de Allende in Mexico. The architecture is characterised by an almost primitive simplicity, conceived as an element in the landscape requiring no maintenance and intended to age like the nature surrounding it. Elemental have designed the lookout point as part of an infrastructure rather than actual architecture: it is one element in a series of small buildings that link the different parts of the pilgrim route. The central concept guiding the lookout point is to provide a resting place offering shade, ventilation, and a view of the pilgrim route. First and foremost a lookout point is somewhere to rest. Distributing the weight of the body with the buttocks above the feet makes sitting on the ground more comfortable. The construction is therefore folded in the middle to form two sloping surfaces. The intention was also to create a cave-like shelter from the sun in the midst of an extremely arid area. Elemental have also addressed the religious aspect of the pilgrim route by inserting a silhouette of the Virgin Mary in the roof: when the sun shines she appears as a shadow on the floor.

Lookout Point Espinazo del Diablo
(The Devil's Backbone)
Design/Construction Period: 2008-2010
Building Area: 148 m^2

Elemental's lookout point is one of numerous stops on the 100 km pilgrim route. The other projects are designed by Ai Wei Wei (Fake Design), Luis Aldrete, Christ & Gantenbein, Dellecamp Arquitectos, Godoylab, HHF, Periférica and Tatiana Bilbao.

The sketch illustrates considerations of view, shade and ventilation, as well as the possibility of creating a resting place at the lookout point.

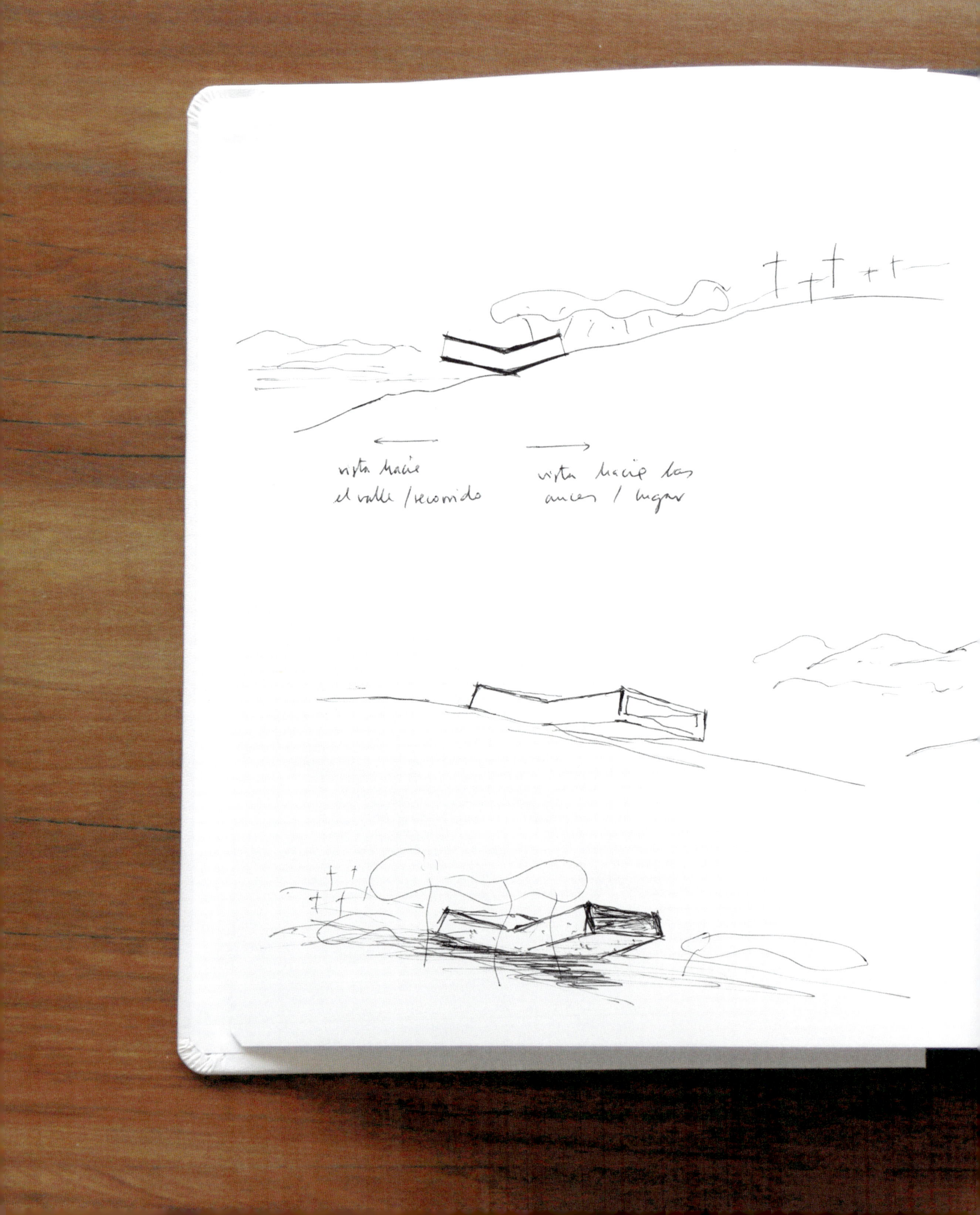

valle

Every year over 2,000 people walk the pilgrim path during Holy Week. The small silhouette of the Virgin Mary has become a popular feature of the route.

de
AMECA

The Art Mill Complex
Doha, Qatar

The highly controlled environment demanded by top art collections often results in a 'blind' box severed from exterior conditions. Elemental, however, did not see such a building fitting in the middle of a spectacular open space by the sea. As they say, what is good for the art might not be good for the city. They decided to create a sloping base for the architecture, celebrating the openness of the site. The mass of the large roof is supported by the mill-like hollow columns. The rhythm of the wide and narrow bays of the grid allows for rooms of different sizes, proportions and heights. Underneath the roof, the structure can provide shafts for technical equipment, stairs, elevators, or smaller exhibition halls. Inside, the silos can provide indirect light as well as expelling hot air, like environmental chimneys. Outside they create a shaded hypostyle promenade with a sense of compression between the silos before opening onto a full view of the ocean. Beyond the silos their rhythm is retained, but the focus is on the space between them, creating an airy structure of light: a kind of forest or souq for the cultural district surrounding the galleries. The water above and shade naturally temper the harsh environment and introduce a more intimate scale. A shared open hypostyle hall marks the entrance to the museum and the cultural district, which is also shared by a mosque bringing the complex into dialogue with everyday life in this part of the city.

Art Mill Complex
Competition Project: 2017 (ongoing)
Building Area: 70,000 m^2

Sketch of the monumental grain silos in which Elemental took inspiration for the Art Mill Complex.

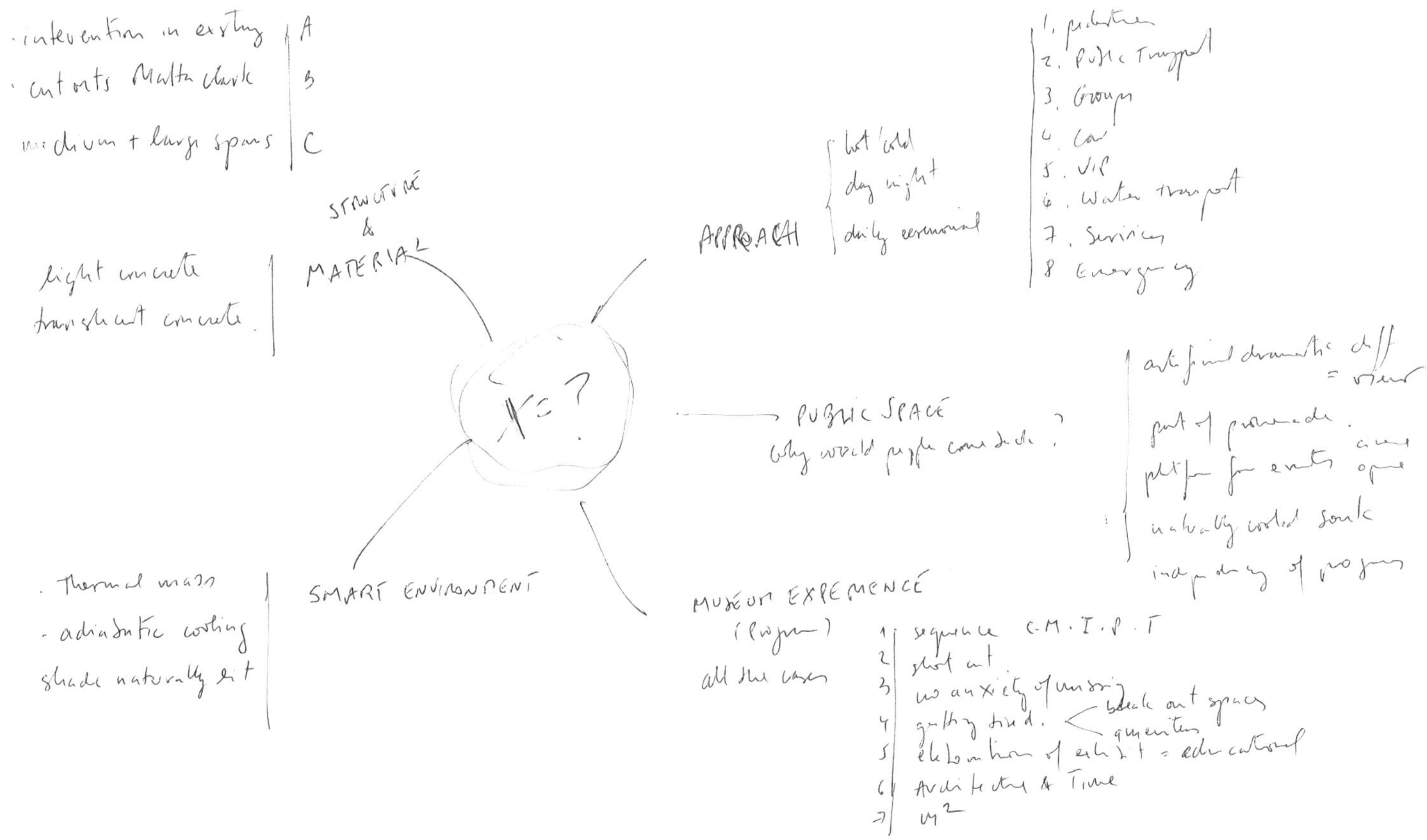
intervention in existing
cut outs Matta Clark
medium + large spans
A
B
C
STRUCTURE & MATERIAL
light concrete
translucent concrete
APPROACH
hot/cold
day/night
daily ceremonial
1. pedestrian
2. Public Transport
3. Groups
4. Car
5. VIP
6. Water transport
7. Services
8. Emergency
PUBLIC SPACE
Why would people come here?
artificial dramatic cliff = views
part of promenade
independency of program
SMART ENVIRONMENT
Thermal mass
adiabatic cooling
shade naturally lit
MUSEUM EXPERIENCE
(program)
all the senses
1 sequence C.M.I.P.T
2 shut out
3 no anxiety of missing
4 getting tired. break out spaces
5 elaboration of exhibit = educational
6 Architecture & Time
7 m2

Not the Answer but the Question: Looking at Constraints and Possibilities in Giving Form to the Built Environment

Interview with Alejandro Aravena
by Michael Juul Holm

MJH: I have heard that you always start the design process by trying to pinpoint the right question to ask. You have said that "there's nothing worse than answering the wrong question well." Can you expand a little on that?

AA: A couple of things can be said about this; in the end, what we do as architects is give form to the places where people live. It's no more complicated than that – and no easier than that. In the end, what we do is find the right form for the built environment. Look outside the window: everything has to have a form. The buildings, the square, the sidewalk, the curb; streets, trees – or no trees? *Where* are the trees, close to the edge, closer to the building? Somebody has to define that form. We don't start by wanting a form in advance – as in having a creative agenda – and then look for a client who'll let us build, say, a round building, because we have an incredible desire to build a round building. We try every time to understand the forces that are at play, informing the task, and these forces change from case to case. Sometimes structure is important, sometimes budget is important, sometimes the environment and the climate are important, sometimes it's the timeframe. Sometimes it's political conditions or social preferences, sometimes it can even be aesthetics, which are *also* among the forces at play. There are usually many forces, sometimes pulling in opposite directions. What we're trying to do is to integrate in one design whatever can consolidate these forces. In social housing there is a need to make an open system, because we just don't have the resources to deliver everything. When there are more resources it's more of – let's say: an ideological thing. We want to make sure that we leave enough room, an open frame for issues or agendas that are not necessarily obvious or important to us. That is what we mean by identifying 'the right question' before jumping to the proper answer. And this capacity to postpone what is wanted until we have posed the question is something that we try to be very rigorous about. I remember having a professor in the 80s at the university who was always thinking in terms like: "You're about to do a tower; what are the two problems of a tower?" As if there were just two. But it was a productive way of working: each project displays a new set of problems that you may choose from or may not even be aware of. But you will be responding to them anyhow, even inadvertently. So in a parallel process we're trying to understand the problems of linear systems, height systems, the mapping of buildings, making deep plans ... and with this total amount of information we try to choose the part of it that is pertinent in the given case. We're trying to arrive at the inevitable core of the given project. Then of course comes the question of form and taste, but that's like handwriting. I write this way, and I can't help it. It comes out that way anyway, and people may recognize a preference for mass or for weight. But because it's almost inevitable, we don't pay attention to it, we focus on the forces at play and on making sure we don't miss any of them.

— So you are refining the equation or the formula?

Yes – for example, we say structure, or budget, or we say climate or function or character. Some of them are very concrete – I can quantify a budget, and it's very clear whether you're within or have overstepped the budget. But take *character* – what is the right character of a building? Even though it's very hard to grasp, it's the first thing you come up against. You come to a building – you don't even know what it is – and you feel uncomfortable, it's ugly, it's ... you know what I mean – there are these intangible dimensions of architecture. Eventually, after identifying the forces at play, any building has to have a structure, but it's not necessarily going to be what really makes the difference to the individual project. That goes from largely concrete constraints to very loose and fluid dimensions. It is a process that in principle never finishes, but we spend a lot of time trying to provide the simplest possible answer to the given set of constraints.

— Something is given when a project starts, like, 'this is a public swimming bath' or 'this is a church'. I guess this defines the beginning of the line of questions or the equation? And, in most cases, you know that it's going to be placed exactly here and not somewhere else ...

Exactly. Those would be some of the variables. I think it's very important, because this is not just responding to what the client would like. Sometimes the client doesn't want or know what's really needed. It is our responsibility to warn them or at least discover it during the process – for example, there might be an issue with noise. Maybe the client wasn't even aware of this; we might have built the house and then found out after a couple of years that it's impossible to live there, because it's too close to a highway. Our task is to identify a force that is not anticipated by the client and make it part of the question before jumping to the solution. In addition, to make the entire process even more challenging, this is not just problem-solving; sometimes it's a question of going into a dimension that wasn't there before. Otherwise, it might be a missed opportunity. Architects are expected, without having to invent a parallel reality, to look at the conditions that gave birth to the question and see if there is a potential for something that was somehow very loosely there, but then becomes an exercise and leads to a position of having succeeded in that project. As with the construction after the earthquake, for example, when there was a need to protect the city against future tsunamis.

— You're talking about Constitución?

Yes, the city of Constitución was going through a reconstruction after the tsunami on 27 February 2010. In the initial participatory process, we understood that one of the things people were expecting was more public space. From the constraints imposed you understand that you can't just spend your money on land excavation; you should also be able to solve the problem of flooding that the city had even without the tsunami. It is your responsibility then to understand that people want to see their new city as something better than what they had before. And identity, the vague question of identity, is very tricky – if you make it simply a cause-and-effect thing, you'll certainly fail. After doing all that, with all the constraints in terms of time and money, if the city that comes out of the process is not better than it was before, that would be a missed opportunity. It is concrete and intangible at the same time. It's problem-solving and responding to a need, but it's also creating a new desire that was not there before your intervention. And this is what we're trying not to invent or make part of our own creative agenda, but to *extract* as a possibility within the set of conditions that we're working in.

— The work in Constitución was quite a multifaceted experience for you as a studio, an experience very different, from what you learned from the Ocean Winery

Michael Martin Juul Holm (b. 1960) is a Danish publisher, critic and editor; 2000-2018 with the Louisiana Museum of Modern Art, now an independant advisor and writer. He has contributed to a nummer of exhibition catalogues and has published architectural interviews with Bjarke Ingels and Julien de Smedt, Renzo Piano, Norman Foster, Cecil Balmond and Francois Roche.

or the experience you had with the stock exchange in Tehran? Over the last 15 years or so you've worked with a lot of quite different tasks – are you going to specialize in something at some point when you have become the best in the world at doing something in particular?

I hope not. It's in our DNA to jump into things that we know very little about. When we started doing social housing, I personally didn't know what a subsidy was. Social housing was a completely unknown field for us, but I guess that, acknowledging our ignorance, we decided to ask the stupid questions that eventually informed the process, and that's no guarantee of success, but eventually it may allow you to move forward. So, we made very rigorous use of our own ignorance, and that has been the case, I guess, over and over again, going into things that we have not done before, like the landfill activity. We had no idea about it, but we asked them to give us all the information they thought might be useful for us even to start defining the question. This wasn't a matter of choice; it was a requirement for reconstruction after an earthquake and a tsunami. So, we do have strategies for tackling the unknown, we are confident in the face of uncertainties; social housing prepares you not only for being okay with losing control, but for understanding the advantage of allowing others access to the system – when you may only be able to channel those forces instead of resisting or controlling them.

What's common to all these things is design. In the end we know that our way of entering into conversations outside our field of knowledge – architecture – is through design. Social housing is something that society can discuss. And so we're interested in social housing as citizens, but the way we enter the conversation in the end is through design.

Reconstruction after an earthquake: everybody would like to discuss reconstruction after an earthquake. But the way we enter that conversation is through design. So we just accept the fact that the starting point is going to be very far from architecture, but we will have to find a way to channel all that information – in the end through form. So I guess we have found a way to cross-pollinate different fields. Social housing is an incredibly powerful filter against the arbitrary. You are given no room, no money, no time to answer all the questions, but it's absolutely necessary to try. You have one nail, one hammer, one hit, and that's it. So instead of complaining about scarcity of resources we appreciate this capacity to be a filter against the superfluous, and we bring this attitude to projects with more inherent resources. Because *reducing* a project is always desirable. If we're going to do a museum or another public building with good funding, we still like the discipline of taking out everything that is not strictly necessary.

UC Innovation Center Anacleto Angelini Santiago, Chile

Although the client had commissioned a glass building, Elemental decided to turn the conventional office plan inside out. The main reason was that the hot climate of Santiago and its direct sunlight on glass surfaces makes the energy consumed by air conditioning soar. Here the contemporary, ubiquitous glass facade of office buildings is replaced by a building where the mass is at the perimeter, with deep recessed openings creating cross ventilation. As a result the energy consumption of the building is one third that of a typical glass tower. The main idea behind the architecture is that innovation and the generation of new knowledge demands encounters and interaction between people. The places where people could meet were therefore multiplied: the standard opaque core was replaced by an open atrium allowing people to see what others are working on, and elevated squares were introduced throughout the height of the building. Finally, the biggest threat to an innovation centre is obsolescence. The architecture here is therefore neutral, making changes in the way it is used over time easy to implement. The monolithic character of the building strives to replace contemporary trends with timelessness. It is a textbook example of the pragmatic inversion of an architectural remit by Elemental: instead of the commissioned glass building, the studio designed a building that would look as heavy as it is. The raw concrete blocks leave us in doubt about scale – object, installation or building? It is not until we get closer that we discover that the hollows are three storeys high.

UC Innovation Center Anacleto Angelini
Design/Construction Period: 2011-2014
Building Area: 8,176 m² (building), 12,494 m² (parking)

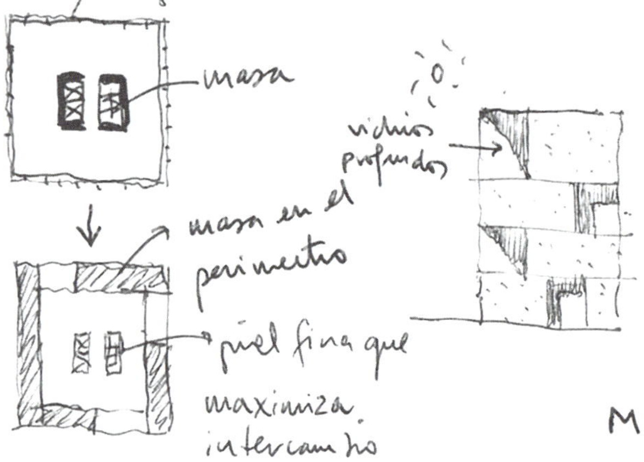

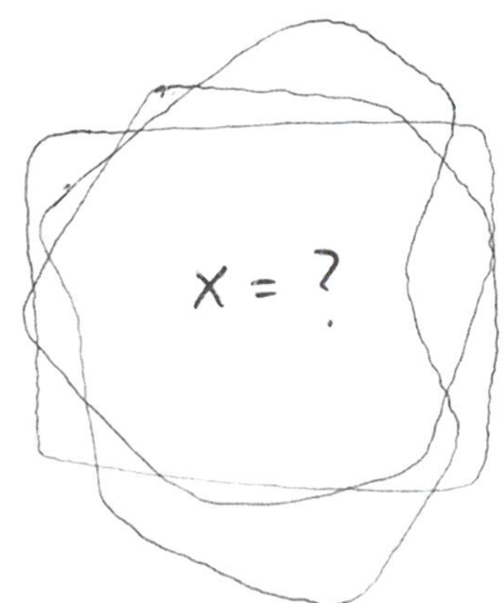

Si bien es un edificio que busca
fomentar el desarrollo → AUSTERIDAD

Si bien es un edificio dedicado
a la innovación → ATEMPORALIDAD

Universidad = creación de conocimiento
Empresa = creación de valor → INSTITUCIONAL

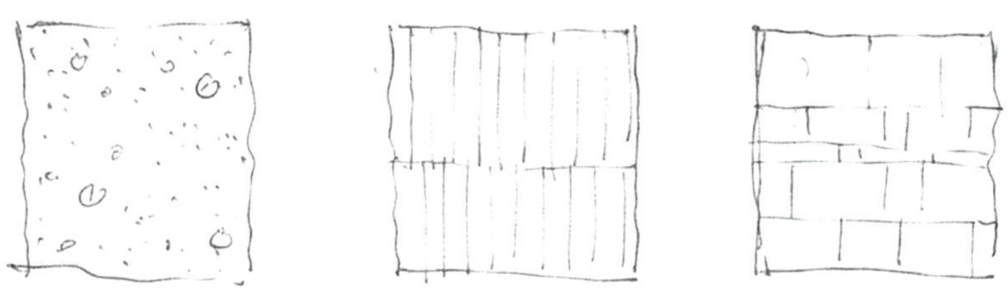

What informs the form of the project?
The 'equation' for UC Innovation Center has numerous variables that shape the project: function, height, innovation, materiality, character, setting, and climate.

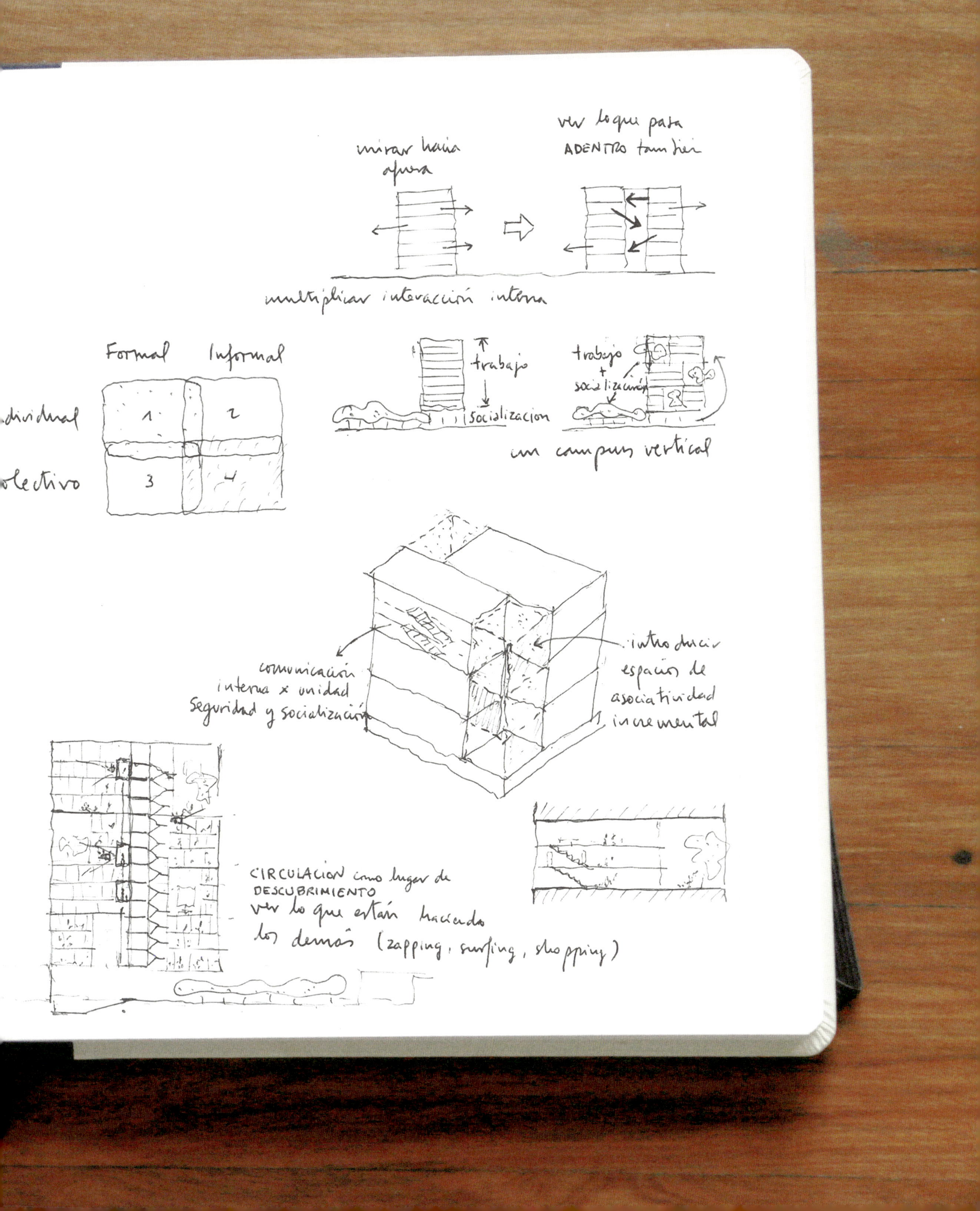

The characteristic three-story windows function as shady courtyards. Due to their depth, the sun never reaches the core of the building.

Bansí Building
Guadalajara, Mexico

Bansí required a building capable of being an icon for the city and at the same time making a contribution to the city's environment by creating free areas. The building should be able to attract and receive urban attention and at the same time remain on the periphery of our attention by providing space for city life. Elemental has taken inspiration from the sculptural qualities of a tree and the way the shadows generated by the tree create a place of rest. A tall tree captures our attention from a distance, but when standing underneath the foliage, the slim trunk frees the view. Bearing this in mind Bansí Building is meant to function both as an icon in the landscape as well as a building, thereby creating space for life in the city by touching the ground at a minimum in order to liberate as much green area as possible. Elemental proposed a facade based on the principles of a foliage. An outer perforated metal skin with 66% porosity around the perimeter prevents the greenhouse effect without sacrificing the transparency in favour of the view and the ventilation of the interior spaces. The windows are placed in a second layer that defines the useful surface of the building, make the slab heads work as eaves giving protection against the sun. All these operations are simply the rigorous use of common sense and the wisdom accumulated by the tradition of constructive practices that are the basis of all notion of sustainability.

Bansí Building
Competition Project: 2009
Building Area: 16,000 m^2

The massive blocks combined with the silhouette of a treetop create very different impressions of the building depending on how and from which angle it is approached.

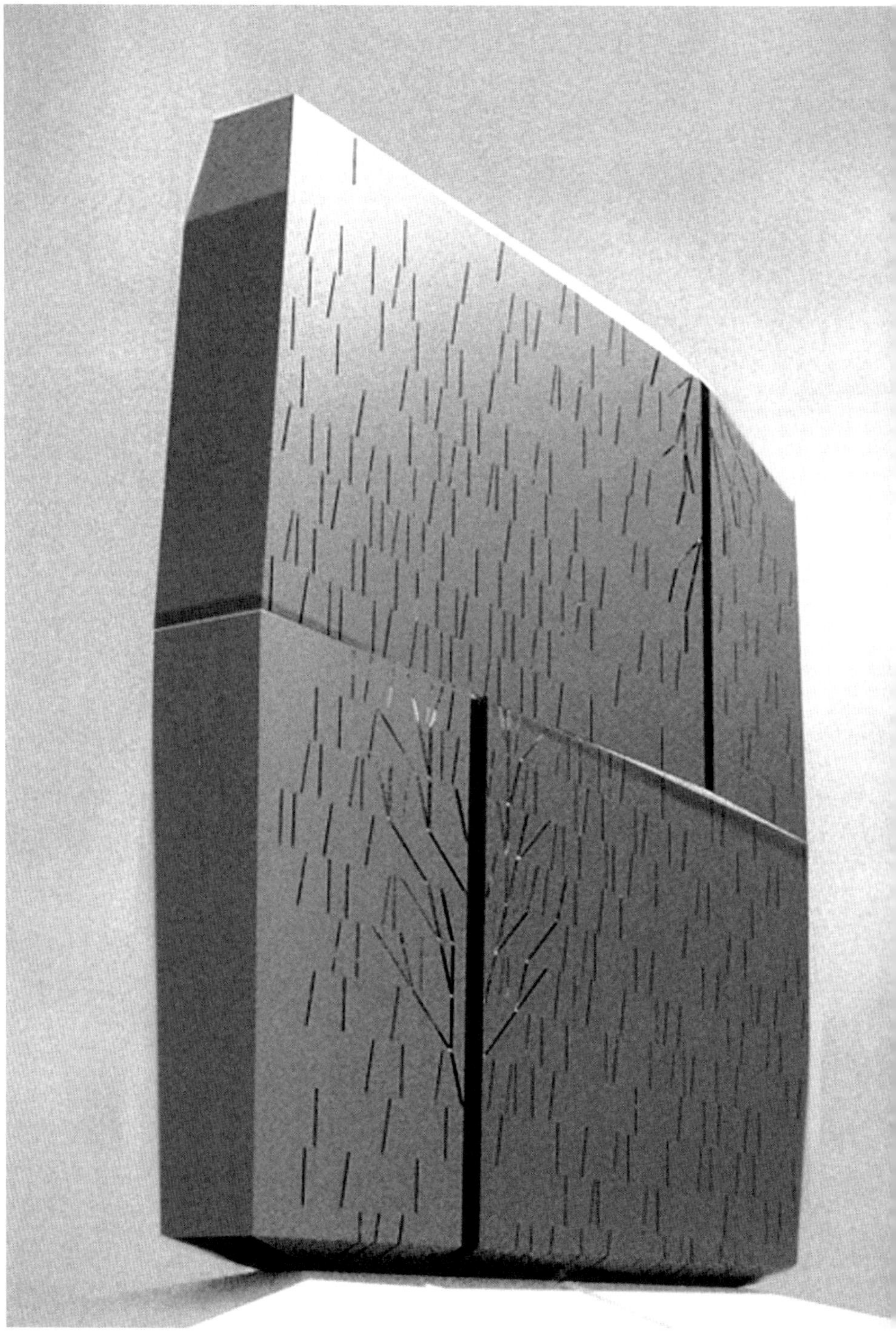

one strong idea.
then don't betray it
with the details & functions.

0 1 5 10

Novartis Shanghai Campus Office Shanghai, China

The office building at Novartis Campus in Shanghai is designed to facilitate different methods of working – individual and collective, formal and informal – and to promote interaction between people. On the ground floor, around a forest of dawn redwoods, a fitness centre and the Be Healthy Centre form part of the public zone on campus where people from the different buildings can meet. A solid facade of reclaimed bricks cover the building to the south, east and west, forming a climate shield. The building is open to the north, allowing indirect natural light to reach the open-plan offices. Using bricks from demolished buildings is traditional in China, creating the characteristic, irregular pattern of used bricks (*wa pan*) seen in old village houses. As well as the obvious sustainability of this use of recycled materials, it also adds the vitality of the irregular and unpredictable traces of human hands to an otherwise potentially static construction.

Novartis Shanghai Campus Office
Design/Construction Period: 2010-2015
Building Area: 3,770 m²

Like a fruit in a husk. Many of Elemental's buildings are based on the concept of a hard, protective exterior and a soft, inviting interior.

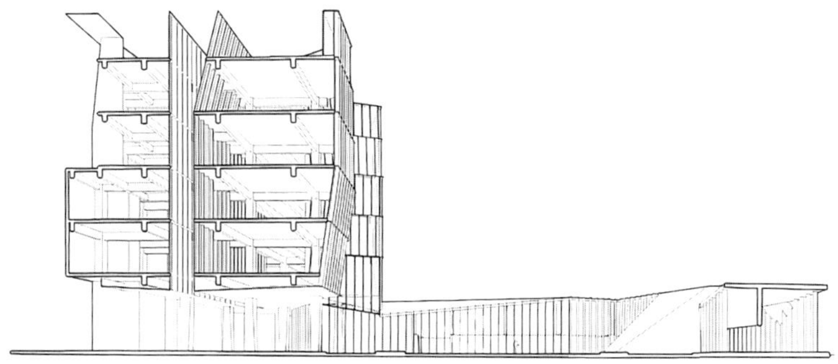

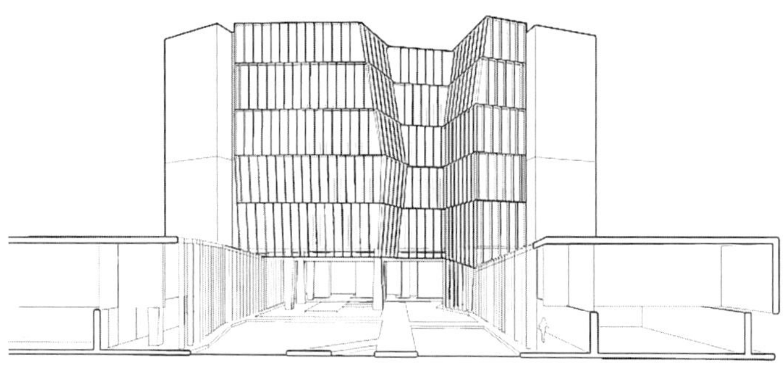

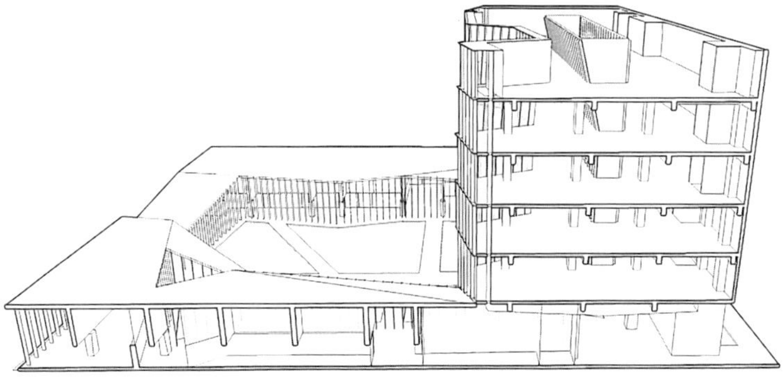

Right: Interior of the ground floor public space. Left: Sorting recycled bricks for the Novartis Shanghai Campus Office being built in the background.

Huara

2017: Huara means star in Aymará, the language of the indigenous people of the Atacama Desert in Chile. The Atacama is one of the darkest deserts on earth, and therefore a place on the planet from which most stars can be seen. The inspiration for this lamp, designed for Italian Artemide, comes from this dark place where humankind can still experience the natural light sources of the stars and moon. The Huara lamp is based on the development of light, from the stars and moon as the only source of light in the dark, to fire, then fuel – first animal fat, then oil and wax – to gas and petroleum, then electric light. It represents a meeting between the first light humankind saw in the sky to the state-of-the-art technology of LED lighting as the latest stage of these developments. The Huara lamp is a flexible light source: the amount of light is determined by the number of zones that are activated.

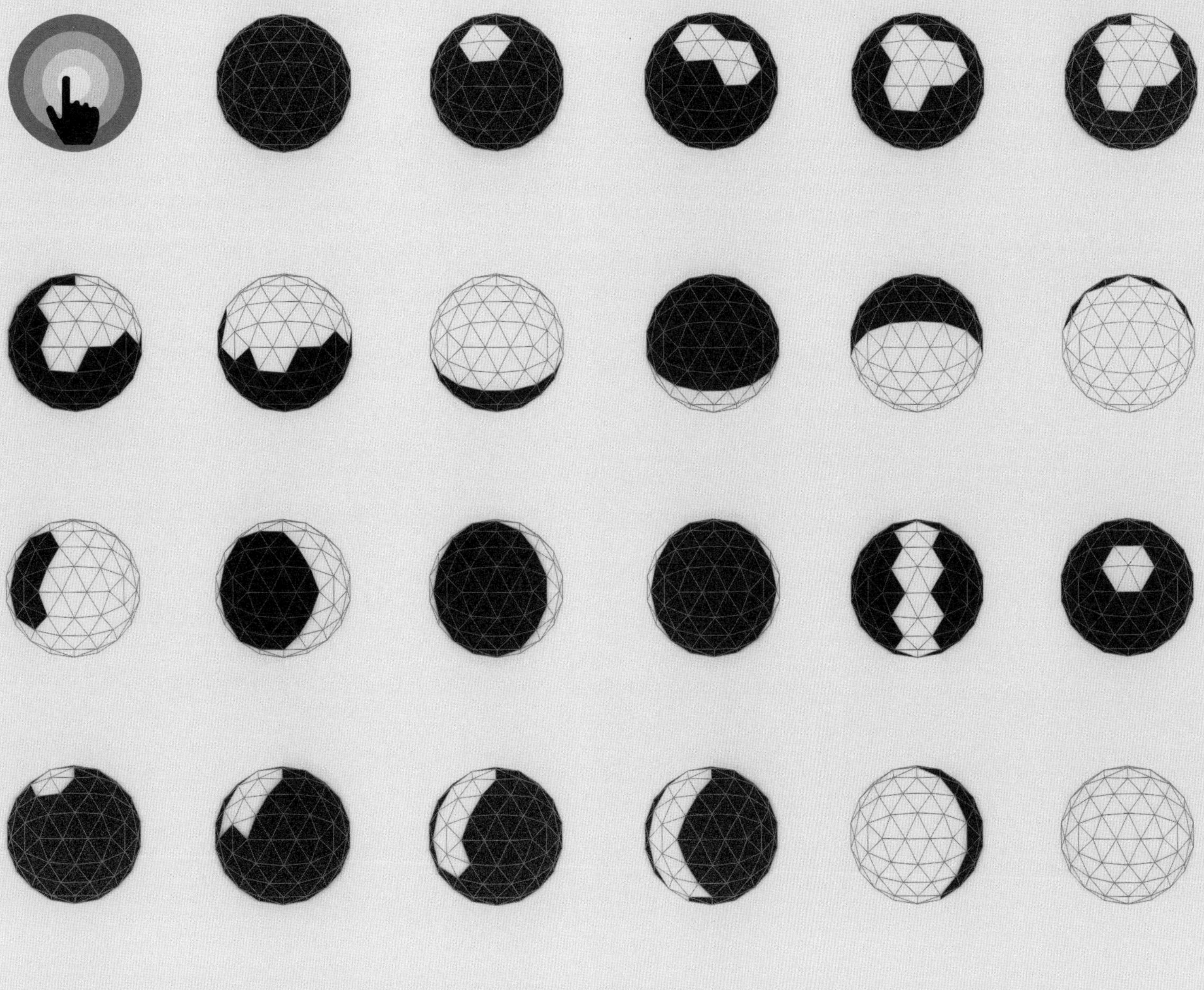

ON THE ROAD
'TILL WE GET THERE
There was nowhere to go but everywhere, so just keep on rolling under the stars.
RUSTIN COHLE
CCTV FOOTAGE 2
TINKER TAILOR SOLDIER SPY

Being Good or Doing Good: Professionalism as a Tool

Interview with Alejandro Aravena
by Michael Juul Holm

MJH: One of the quite central elements in your practice is the social aspect: social housing, social architecture and planning for cities. Or perhaps a better word to use is altruistic. *Social in this context usually describes projects that do something for the masses or the poor, in the sense of doing somebody a favor. While* altruistic *is more like making the most of what we have and doing it together. How do you respond to this?*

AA: I can agree to the word altruistic. But I would put it differently – the word that comes to my mind, more than any, is the word *challenging*. Creating a fair built environment where the common good can be guaranteed and balanced with individual gains, that is a real challenge. And more than good will or charity, it very much requires professional *quality*. I think that from the very beginning – I am now going back to the year 2000, when the subject, social housing, was so fraught, and there was a lot of guilt around, a kind of morally superior attitude was expected from anybody working in the public sector or on programs for the poor. For our part we were very clear in saying that not even for a second did we claim any kind of ethical superiority. We are not particularly good people. Without any false modesty, we think we're good designers. And in design there is a very powerful tool, which is *synthesis* – the most needed resource for handling complexity. So we thought that to tackle an issue that was difficult, we might contribute and engage in that conversation with some tools that were required, urgent and pertinent to such a complex issue.

But not as any kind of social 'good deed'. It was important not to let this become a moral issue, not to make others feel guilty about not doing the same. But it was also of pragmatic importance. If you claim any kind of moralistic approach, then you shouldn't be charging a fee while working for the poor, not even in an altruistic way. Of course, you can always choose how to spend your time: creating social housing or public space, or working with reconstruction after natural disasters. But there's no question that if society doesn't change its attitude to the common good as something that we'll be doing with the leftovers – if we do not put it at the centre of our interest – then we won't make changes that benefit everybody.

— When it comes to social housing, one of the 'tools' that you use is the participation of the people who are going to live in these buildings. You have worked like that several times and in different ways, such that in one case you built what has been labeled 'half a house', meaning that in the other half only the bearing walls and slabs are there, while anything else has to be added by the people themselves. And in other cases, it's more as if there is a house, and then the residents can add to it or put something into it. What is your experience with that?

I think it's a very important question and I'm glad that we have the opportunity to clarify once again. Evidence shows that a middle class family, which is most of us, would live reasonably well in 80 m^2. But evidence *also* shows that with public money it is impossible to build more than 40 m^2. It's a fact that wherever you go in the world the public sector – in the best of the cases, working at the best of its capacity, with state of the art technology – can only deliver 40 m^2. And with that fact in mind, you can choose to do what markets do, which is to deliver what ends up being a small house of 40 m^2, and then a family can build on top of that until they achieve the middle class standard, *despite* design, not *thanks to* design. Or you can do what we tried to do, namely look at those 40 m^2 as half of the good house that everybody would like to have, including ourselves, and reframe the problem as delivering the half that cannot be achieved *individually*. The starting point is again absolutely pragmatic, beginning with what the evidence shows. You go to an informal settlement, to a slum – you're a poor family in a developing country, which is a reality for two billion people in the world. You get a housing solution of around 40 m^2, make it grow, and the process stops around 80 m^2. Acknowledging that we cannot deliver what is going to happen anyway – at a formal level or even with illegal approaches – we just reframe the problem and accept it. What we do is, we are very precise in designing what hasn't been built yet: the second half, those square meters that are going to be built anyhow, and we channel them within the framework we have laid down. We made the families' lives easier and safer, and made it cheaper to achieve the middle class standard. It started as a cold-blooded, pragmatic approach, but eventually over time we learned that there were situations where we had funding to build more square meters. The feedback we got from the participatory process was that you don't simply separate resources and responsibilities, you also have to understand what the 'clients' expect from the operation, what their real needs are, their desires. During that process we understood that even if the money were there, they would still have wanted governments or markets to leave some room within a generic framework for adaptation to their individual realities.

Families differ greatly. Some have many children and need more rooms, others want to run a business at home, some have animals, others again want to park a car inside their house – and it's impossible at a centralized level to incorporate such levels of diversity. What started as a reaction to scarcity was soon reframed as the need and desire to respond with an open system: Something that allows individual initiatives to be channeled through the structural framework, without threatening the common good. We could have provided even less – just the frames, slabs and columns, and then allowed it to be filled in randomly over time. But that would have been a threat to the common good. We wanted to balance framing with something that can guarantee the quality of the shared urban exterior, yet allows for individual intervention. I guess in the end what we are now more conscious of – what started as a pure need and a reaction to a lack of resources – is a tool that transforms scarcity into growth. If you can't do everything, focus on what's difficult and what cannot be done privately and individually. At the same time, provide a system that is loose and open, so what you can't know in advance can enter into the system and adapt to tastes, preferences and sensibilities.

It is important to highlight the fact that the participatory process plays a role not only in completing the house, but also in defining the best way to spend the money in the first half, by making the priorities clear. In some projects we came with a preconceived idea that this or that might be more important for the family at the first stage; but during the participatory process we came to realize that other things were more important – for instance a water heater versus a bathtub. We all thought that anyone would prefer a water heater over a bathtub, but they said, counterintuitively, "No, the bathtub!" The bathtub can be used for a more diverse range of purposes and they would be able to buy a water heater and get it installed later. An important part of participatory design is that it helps us define exactly what the question is before we try to close in on an answer. If anybody knows how to make the most strategic use of scarce resources and establish priorities, it's the family.

We involve them in the process because there is a knowledge they have, a capacity to decide very quickly, a kind of street wisdom that tells you what is most important. When you're integrating with them they expect you to preserve a certain dignity in the way you treat them, whoever you are, on the state side or as a professional. They must not be treated as 'the poor' who have had to get help because they're incapable. They are asked to contribute with what they *do* have. They may not have money, but they have other things to offer in a difficult situation. And this process has created a lot of respect. This is not just a romantic thing. We treat them with a lot of respect, although we don't do everything they may want. In a participatory process they may ask for things that make no sense, and we have no problem saying no. This is our professional responsibility. We don't feel any kind of guilt because they're poor, none of the parties claim any kind of moral superiority. I guess that over time this creates a civic relationship: it's instructive for us, but also for the people that we're working with.

— How does the participatory process start, practically?

Number one: With information and the communication of constraints. When we did our first project in the public sector, it meant a subsidy of 7,500 USD with which we had to buy the land on the private market, do the infrastructure – water, sewage, electricity – and build the house. So, in aggregate it was one third for each part of the process. With 2,500 USD to buy a piece of land, the only kind you can afford is land in the periphery – that is, a periphery where's there's nothing but housing, which is a tragedy. People come to cities looking for opportunities of jobs, for education, health care, transportation and recreation: in these peripheries there's none of that. You're really far away and segregated from the opportunities that made you come to the city. So in 2001 they changed to a 10,000 USD policy in which families were getting a 3,200 USD subsidy and the rest was a loan with a private banking system. There are two problems with that. First, the solutions you got for 10,000 USD were so bad that families stopped paying. If I buy a TV on credit that is not working, I stop paying – and the same thing happened to housing, to a point where 70% of the beneficiaries were not paying back the loan! This of course was unsustainable for the whole system, and in the long run it would have led to bankruptcy. And the other problem was that it was not targeting the really poor. When you're poor, the notion of monthly payment doesn't make any sense. It's not that the poor don't have money, but they don't have money coming in the form of monthly payments. So they're invisible to the banking system. It was an unfocused policy. In order to correct that, a new policy was created that doubled the subsidy – it went from 3,200 USD to 7,200 USD, with no debt. But the final amount was less: from 10,000 USD it went down to 7,500 USD. And it required 300 USD of savings from each family. It can take them a couple of years to save up a sum like that; it's not easy to save when you are in survival mode! So even though in terms of public policy the subsidy was bigger, the sum total was in fact less. That was the system of rules at the time, and we decided to see if we could do something with that set of rules.

As part of that policy, one of the conditions was that families had to be incorporated into the process, because it was known that with even less money it was going to be impossible to deliver a real housing solution. Actually, the name of that first policy in Spanish was *Vivienda Social Dinámica sin Deuda*, meaning Dynamic Social Housing without Debt. The dynamic condition, the fact that people themselves were going to contribute to it, was already kind of anticipated, because what you could deliver with public money was not going to be enough. It was the municipality that would eventually organize people so that they would be part of the project. It could take the form of an NGO or a building company. They wanted to get the subsidies, they just had to deliver a design with the stamp of a participatory process. The participatory process was then just signing a paper saying that you had gone to a meeting; the company would say we will start in March and deliver in December – "sign here, that's participatory design, done!"

We had to invent what a participatory process really was, in a very rudimentary and improvised way. What are the questions, what are you expecting from us? It's an anxious and emotional thing: it's the first time that they have had an architect, a professional working for them. Actually, in the history of social housing, you never knew the architect in any country. In this case you have face-to-face contact with your designer. And the other way around. Usually as an architect, if you have some big company or wealthy person giving you a job, you have a discussion. But if you're doing something for hundreds of people, you don't. Another thing that we learnt, and had to learn very quickly, was never to specify the number of square meters that you're going to deliver. From the design process you'll have more or less value engineering and can say that with this amount of money and with this amount of land I'm going to be able to deliver 36 m^2. If, between then and paying the current market price of the steel or concrete, you are able to deliver only 35, that's just another promise that has been broken. We were careful to say, just in terms of rooms: "Your house will have one bathroom, one kitchen, living room, dining room, one bedroom." Then you can adjust if the shit hits the fan. It happens all the time: the system is so fragile. On the one hand the clients were very skeptical: "Why should I trust the state or the market that has always neglected us?" At the same time they have expectations, and if we create expectations that we can't meet, it creates a social time bomb that is very difficult to manage afterwards.

If you plan housing in an environment where there is no real society around it, what actually happens to it?

Well, there *is* a society, because in order to go from being invisible to being visible to the formal system – in order to get a house – networks are created spontaneously. As soon as you go into these informal environments, networks are created to support your social disadvantages. You have the notion of the extended family, for example: you're living together with grandparents, nephews, cousins, uncles. It's not the nuclear family as we know it, it's a much bigger group. There are strategies that we have to translate into space, rather than merely creating small apartments. The family that gets the subsidy may look like a normal family – what is invisible to the system is that they're more distant relatives. And unless you create a spatial translation of that, something is missing. That's why the courtyard, for example, around which 20 to 25 families live, is something that came out of these self-organized social structures. It was them telling us: Look, we are not 100 families, nor are we just each a family on its own. We're this smaller group: some are relatives, some have cultural connections or form an ethnic group. Now with the new immigrants from Haiti or Peru or wherever, these kinds of clusters form more often: Networks of families or friends, or people just linked by their former country. And actually people themselves were complaining that the networks created out of necessity in order to get the house then disappeared because there was no spatial correlation that meant they had to be maintained. After you got your house, there were still so many problems to be solved that it would have been desirable to keep the networks together. Who would take care of the children, if a couple went out to work? In a conventional housing project grandparents are separated from the parents and thereby also from the grandchildren. Then when the network disappears, one of the two parents has to stay at home and the income is reduced to half. You want to go back to that informal reality, because in terms of social support it was more efficient. It was important to allow for this and translate it into a form that upheld the social structure.

— When it comes to the finishing of the houses, the participation in the building process itself, do people also organize in working groups – do they do things for each other?

During the construction process we continue with the participating parties to communicate how they can 'grow' their new home. During the construction process they prepare, they start to get more material like paint, or just decide what kind of building they want. We have a participatory program working with paper models, showing what kind of architecture they will have and what kind of expansion they can do. This explains why expansion often happens so quickly after they get a house, because they've been thinking about it or have actually saved money for it over the last months of the construction phase. So they get the house, and two weeks later they know what to do, and it's finished. Everything's very simple: it's mostly finishing – some partition walls – but minor things compared to the general structure of the house. It's very cheap, but obviously it depends on the resources of the individual family.

— In some of the early settlements in the United States, when Christian communities were moving west, once they had arrived at a place where they wanted to settle, first they built a house for Mr. Henderson, then they built a house for the Peterson family, and so on – everyone was engaged in working on the other people's houses ...

What has happened here, and I think it's something that we somehow knew or intuitively guessed, is described by the Peruvian economist Hernando de Soto in the book *The Mystery of Capital*. He studied informal settlements and proved that the amount of money in slums is quite considerable. If I want to buy a house in a favela in Rio de Janeiro, it's not cheap: I will need 40-50,000 USD. It's an average middle class market, but since it's informal and there are no valid property documents for what you are acquiring, the asset cannot have a life as capital: you cannot use it as an economic tool in your life, it's only a shelter from the environment. What we knew through this kind of study is that people had money, so the process of making the initial house grow to its middle class potential is not necessarily something that people do with their own hands. It was a process that took a long time, since there is no monthly income. But all of a sudden they may get what in a more general sense we can call resources: A load of bricks – we don't even want to ask how they got there – but they have bricks. Or money. What happened is that, more than building with their own hands, they were hiring workers to work on their homes. Now they are willing to spend money on their houses. In the previous condition, when they were not formal owners of the land, there was always the risk of being evicted. So if they had money, they had it in the form of a TV the size of a wall that you could take with you, or sneakers. Things that are not going to be lost if they're evicted. The moment their property rights are guaranteed, all that money goes into the house. What we did during the construction process was to identify possible builders. And this is another outcome of the participatory process. Normally people come from the construction industry, they are masons or carpenters. Filling the void, we trained them to draw up a budget for the second half of the house, because there was no material loss – what you'd need is a wooden beam of the exact size sold in Chile, a steel beam cut in half, no waste of material, and plaster panels. We helped them to adjust, so they could offer stuff to the other families: "Would you like the next 36 m^2 of your house? I can give it to you for 2,000 USD." It was a rather efficient operation, one house after another: they knew exactly how much plasterboard, how many nails, how many beams they would need for the expansion. It created a small industry of people who knew about construction.

In this way, even the technological transfer of giving training to workers that we identified in the community was part of the participatory process. For social housing, the way we enter into the dialogue, going back to your first question, is not through morality, it's through design. We have been training our 'designer muscles' in the other projects, so that when we have to depart from architecture, we already have our muscles tensed. We know exactly what each technique can deliver. And that's absolutely necessary for the other business.

Tehran Stock Exchange
Tehran, Iran

The building in Tehran had to meet two demands that were not easy to reconcile: being accessible to the public, at the same time as offering a high level of security. The building plot was narrow, and the distribution of the space predefined: a large hall on the ground floor with conventional floors of offices above. The brutally monolithic facade closes the building to the outside world, but inside it opens onto several inner courtyards. The triangular grid of the ground plan made it possible to move weight and load-bearing structures to the outer walls, freeing up space inside. The outer walls also slope slightly upwards, making the building earthquake-proof. The building has several Elemental hallmarks: the monolithic facade and softer inner courtyards; a facade creating niches that allow natural light into an increased number of interior spaces; social meeting points throughout the building; and hollows in the facade, some of which extend over several floors. Due to the trade embargo on Iran, that has stopped imports, local instead of imported building supplies and construction techniques were used. The traditional ceramics industry of northern Iran supplied the bricks that form an interlaced pattern on the north and south facade, preventing direct sunlight entering the building and thereby reducing the inside temperature and the energy consumed by air conditioning.

Tehran Stock Exchange
Project: 2012
Building Area: 30,000 m^2

looking up the shape of the atrium moves from concave to convex

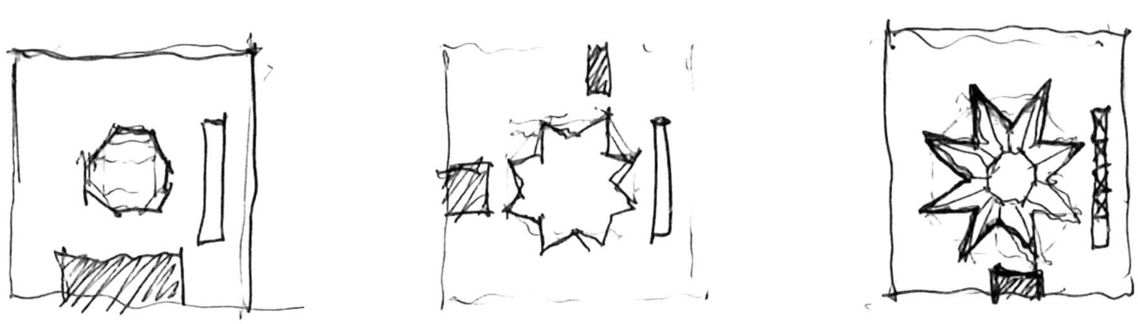

lower floor starts as octagon — upper floor the sides become a star

Sketches exploring the atrium that starts as an octagon and ends in a star shape.

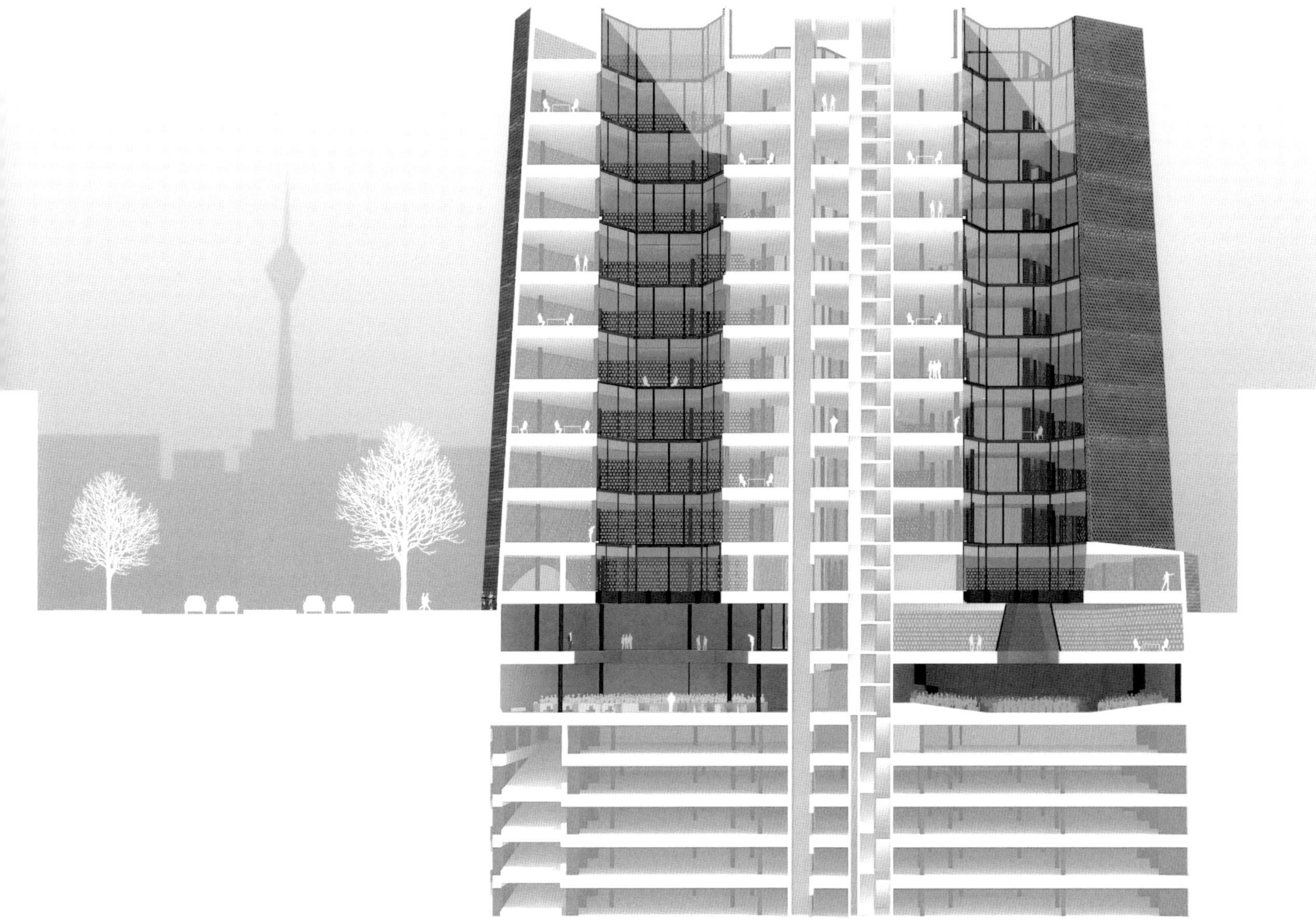

The small building plot and pre-established distribution of m² between the basement, ground floor and other levels generated the idea of splitting the building into multiple, interconnected blocks. This allows sunlight into all the rooms on the lower floors.

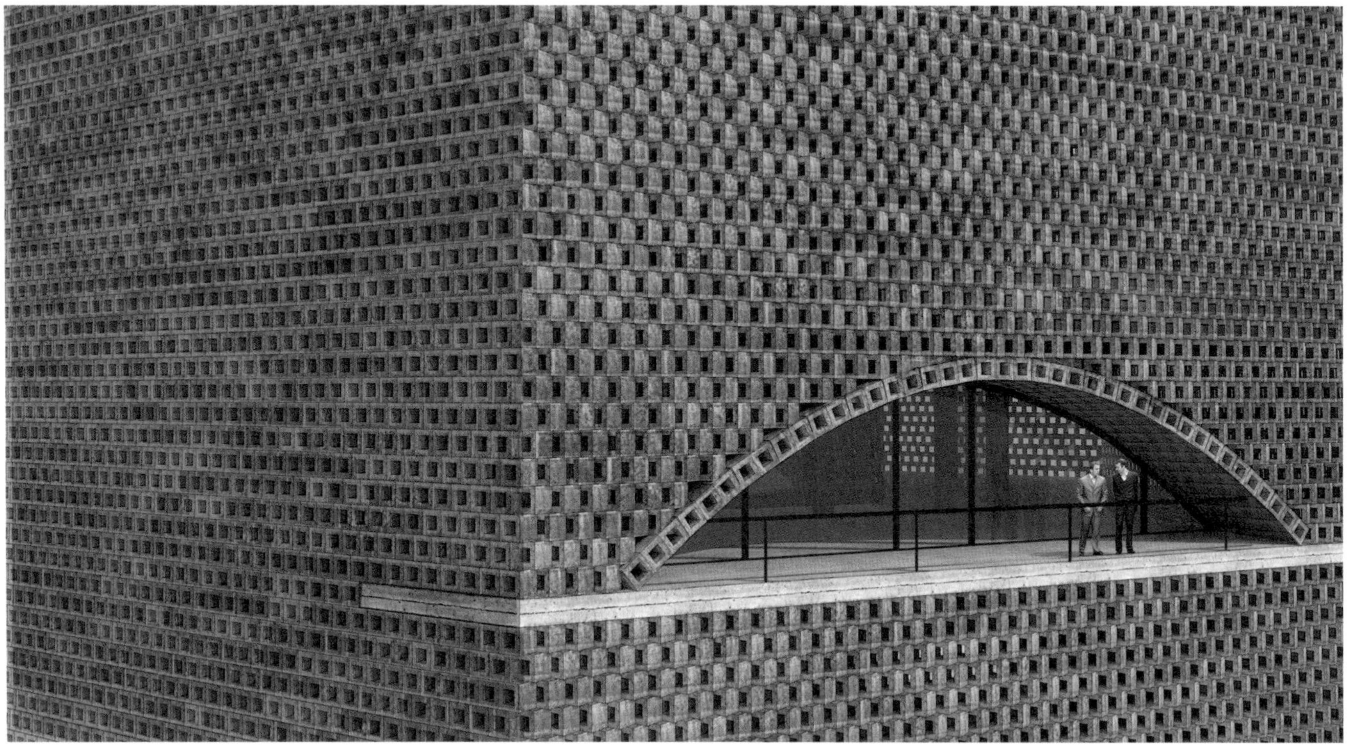

Fig 1

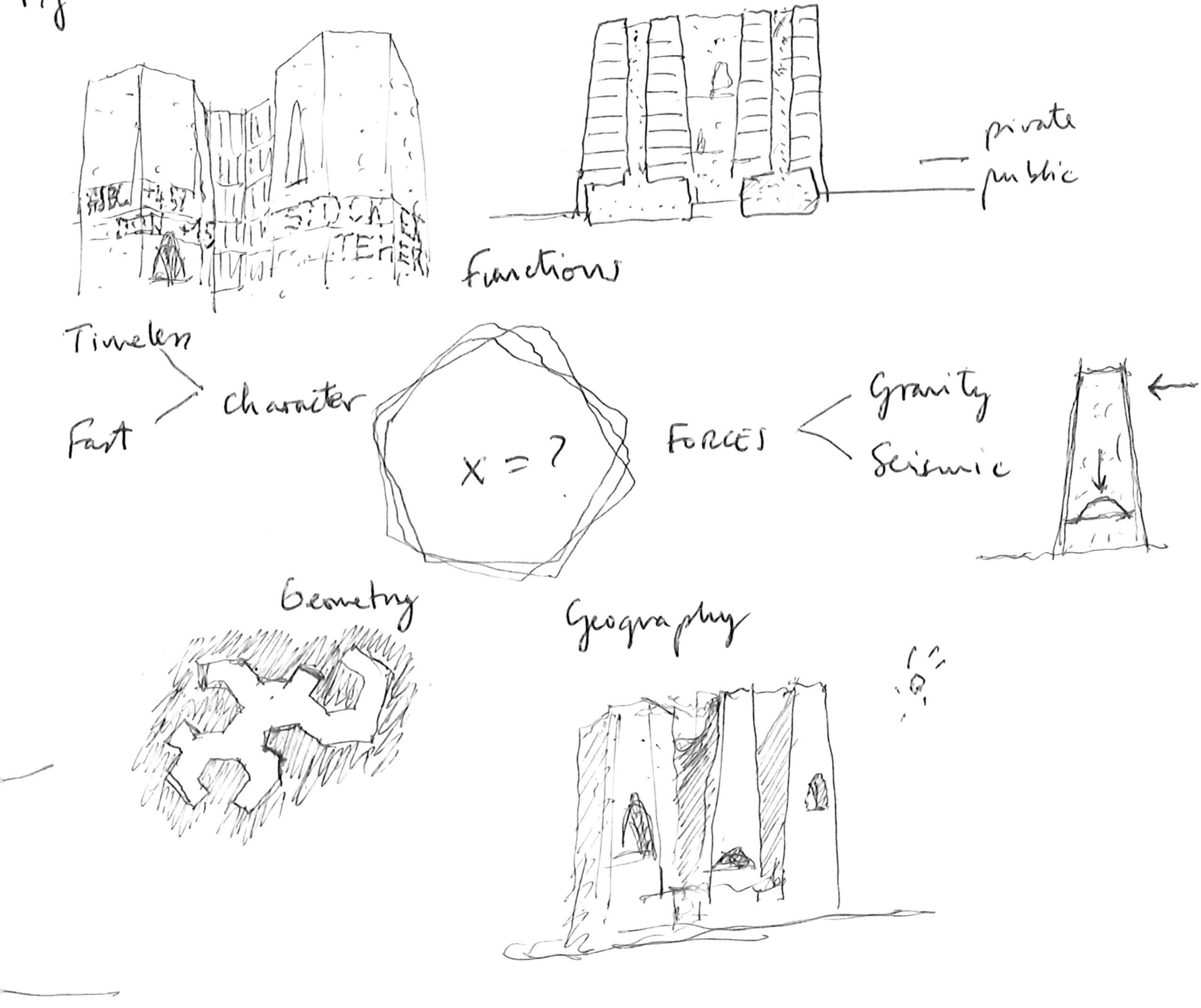
Functions
private
public
Timeless
character
Fast
x = ?
Forces
Gravity
Seismic
Geometry
Geography

The ABC of Incremental Housing

By ELEMENTAL

Of the three billion people living in cities today, one billion live under the poverty line. By 2030 two billion of the five billion people who will be living in cities will be under the poverty line. That means we will have to build a city for a million people per week at a cost of 10,000 USD per family. Given the magnitude of the housing shortage, we won't solve this problem unless we add people's own resources and building capacity to that of governments and the market. And this is why we thought of putting in place an *Open System* that can channel all the available forces in play. That way people will be part of the solution, not part of the problem.

It is however a fact that the available resources, in terms of time and money, are not enough. To face such a scarcity of resources the market tends to do two things: Reduce and Displace. Reduce the size of the houses threatening the quality of life of their inhabitants, and displace them to underserved peripheries where land costs nothing, segregating people from the opportunities that made them come to cities in the first place. In order to face scarcity we propose a principle of *Incrementality*.

If as an architect you can't do everything, focus on:

A. What is more difficult

B. What cannot be done individually by the residents

C. What will guarantee the common good in the future

We identified five design conditions as *The ABC of Incremental Housing*:

1 Good location: projects dense enough to pay for expensive, well located sites.

2 Harmonious growth in time: build the first half strategically (partition structure and firewalls, bathroom, kitchen, stairs, roof) so that expansion can take place thanks to the design, not despite it. Frame individual performances and actions so we get a customization instead of a deterioration of the neighborhood.

3 Urban layout: introduce, between private space and public streets, collective space for no more than 25 families, so that social harmony can be maintained.

4 Provide structure for the final scenario of growth, not just for the initial one.

5 Middle-class DNA: plan for a final scenario of at least 72 m^2 or 4 bedrooms (3x3 m), with space for a closet or double bed. Bathrooms should not be by the front door, the typical solution to save on pipes, but where the bedrooms are. They may include a bathtub, not just a shower receptacle, and space for a washing machine. There should be space for parking a car. None of this is even close to the case in social housing nowadays.

The following projects pursue the goals and principles of *Incremental Housing*.

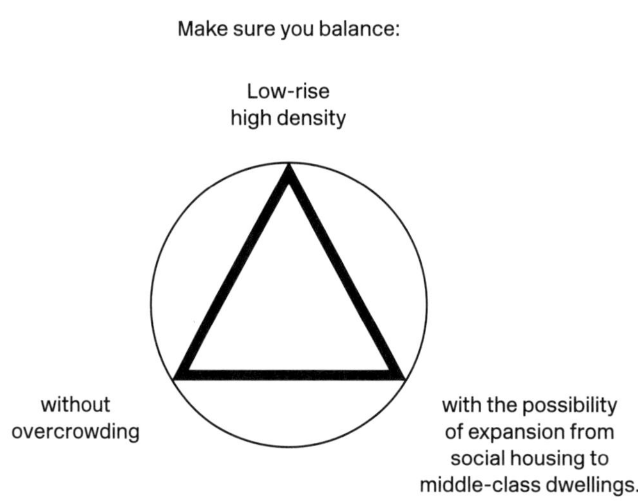

1st 50% = US$ 7,500

2nd 50% = US$ 750

US$ 7,500 + US$ 750 = US$ 20,000

Quinta Monroy
Iquique, Chile

The challenge of Elemental's first project was to accommodate a hundred families using a subsidy of 7,500 USD that in the best of the cases allowed for 36 m² of built space in a 5,000 m² site, which cost three times what social housing could normally afford. 60% of the inhabitants had no light or direct ventilation, no running water or sewer connection. Each family occupied an average of 30 m² in dwellings built from the refuse of shipping materials from the port. Crime and drug trafficking were facilitated by the labyrinth-like nature of the compound. None of the solutions in the market solved the equation. Elemental thought of a typology where the buildings could make very efficient use of land and the houses allowed for expansion. After a year, each property value was beyond 20,000 USD. Still, all the families have preferred to stay and continue improving their homes, instead of selling them. The design of Quinta Monroy was not much different from the normal housing concrete block boxes available. Better design does not mean decoration or aesthetics, but the strategic use of form achieving enough density to pay for well-located land, without overcrowding and with the capacity to manage growth.

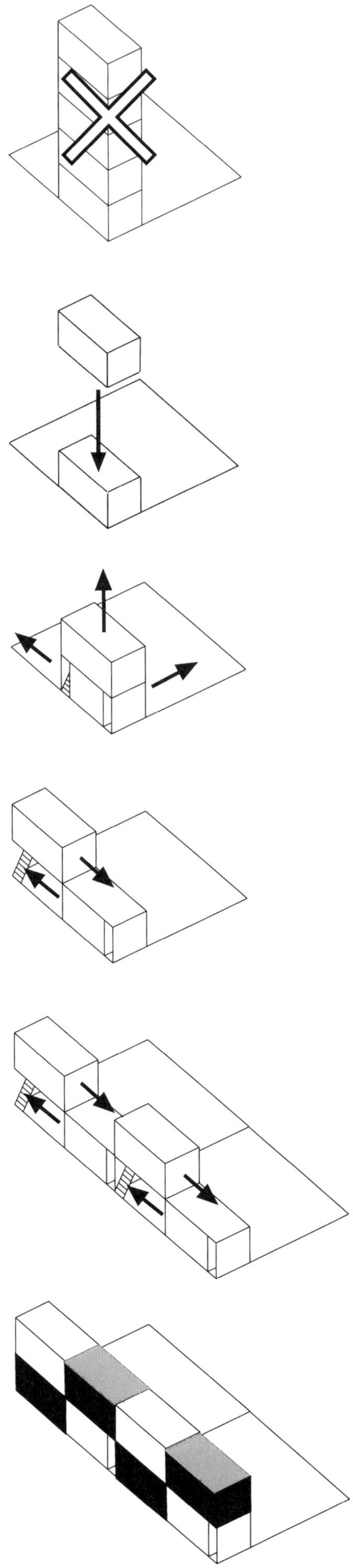

Design/Construction Period: 2003-2004
Building Area: 3,620 m² (93 House Complex)
Initial House: 36 m²
Expanded House: 70 m²
Initial Apartment: 25 m²
Expanded Apartment: 72 m²
Density: 162.5 Houses/ha

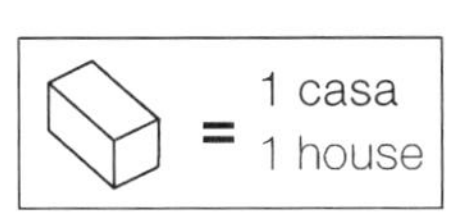

Opposite page: The concept of The Parallel Building is a building with just a ground and a top floor: a house running parallel to an apartment above: An updated version of the typical colonial Latin America two-story house with two doors for each lot facing the street: one door leading to the house and the courtyard, the other opening to a staircase leading to the upper floor unit. Elemental's contribution was to make the house "porous" allowing the expansions to occur in the "pores."

Aerial view before (top) and after (bottom).

Top: Existing housing typology of the market.
Bottom: The original condition of the area.

Top: December, 2004. Bottom: June, 2006

Las Anacuas
Monterrey, Mexico

In the Mexican housing market, the cheapest solution that is offered costs about 30,000 USD. So the poor are not being reached. Elemental developed an improved version of Iquique where houses underneath and duplex apartments on top have an initial cost of 20,000 USD, but can achieve a middle-income standard of 72 m^2 after self-built expansions. The efficiency in land use without overcrowding made it possible to purchase land in a neighborhood where the average cost is 50,000 USD. The families were expected to benefit from that value gain and from the fact that the cost of land reflects close availability of services and opportunities. To be able to house 70 families on a site of 6,600 m^2, Elemental designed a building that occupied the entire perimeter of the rectangular lot, but leaving room for a central collective space.

Example of housing typologies developing in the market at the time.

Design/Construction Period: 2008-2009
Land Area: 6,591 m^2 (70 House C omplex)
Initial House: 40 m^2
Final House: 76,6 m^2
Initial Duplex: 40 m^2
Expanded Duplex: 76,6 m^2
Winner of INDEX AWARD, Home Category, Denmark, 2011

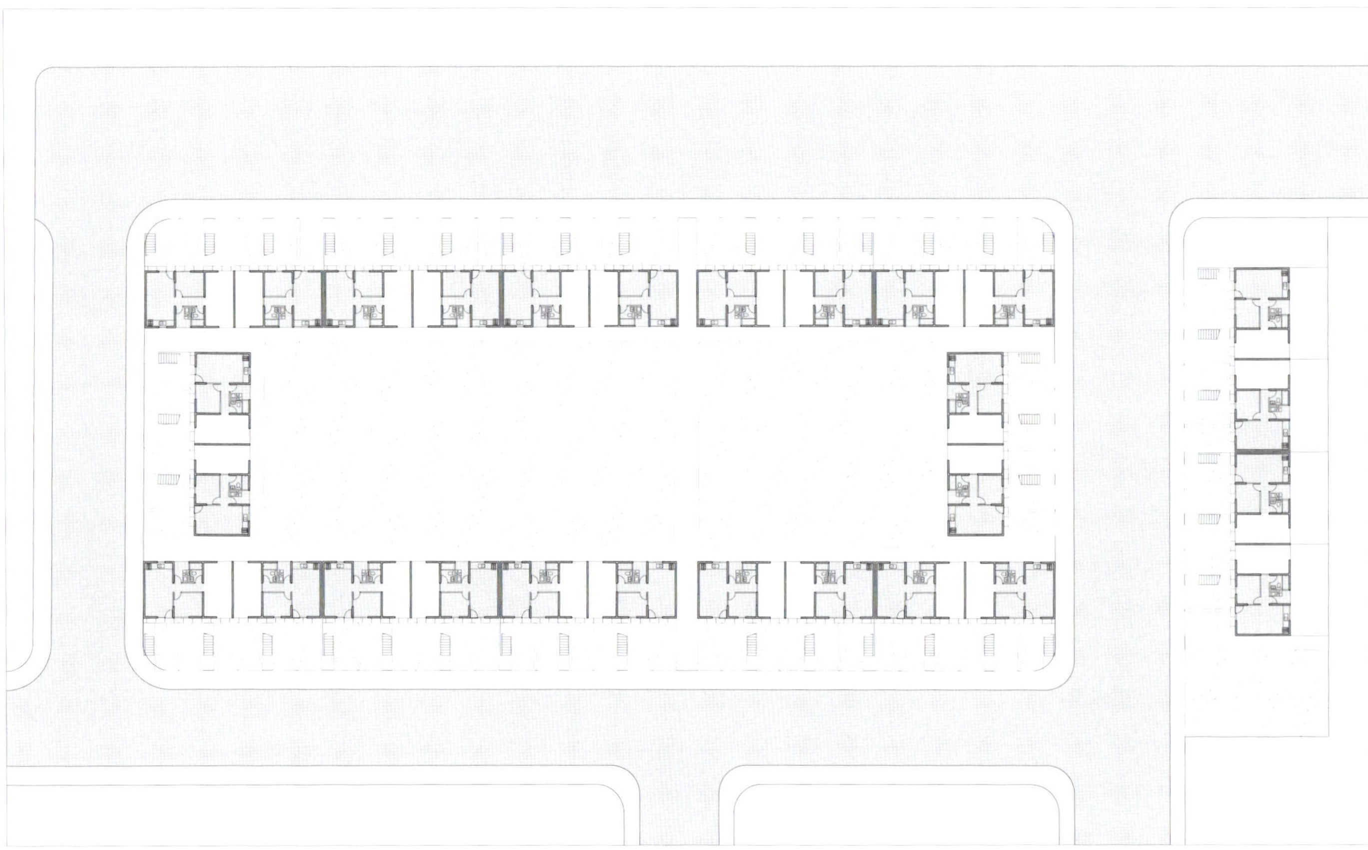

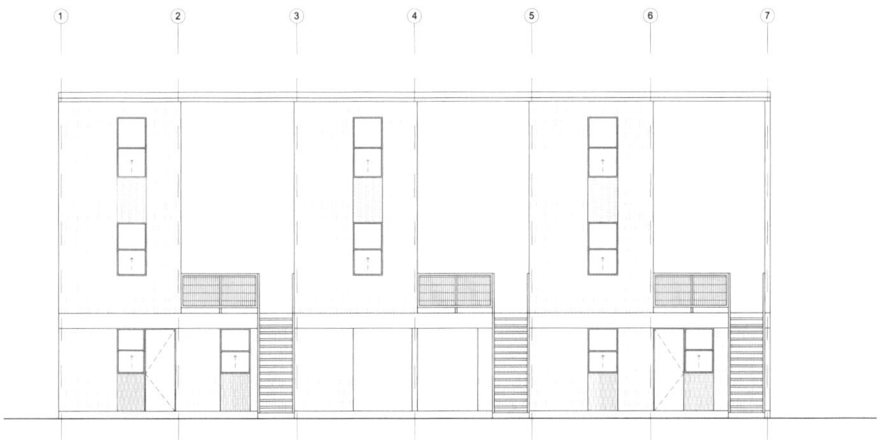

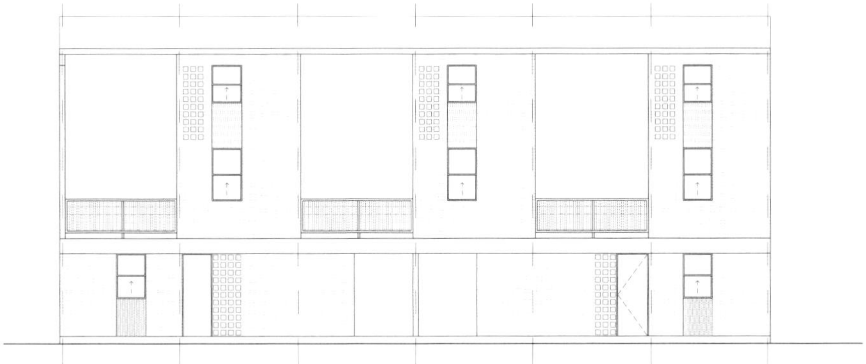

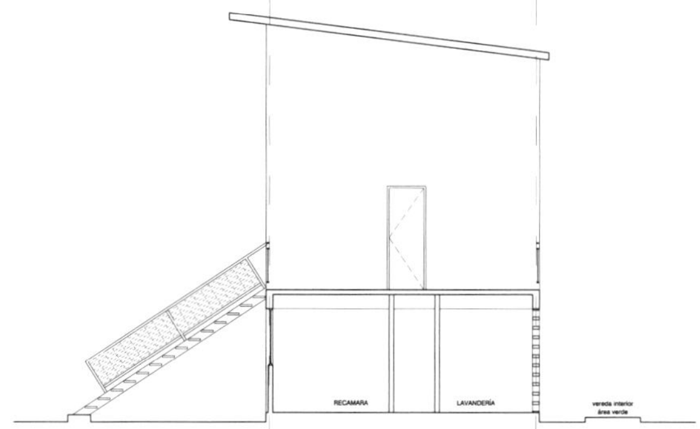
RECAMARA
LAVANDERIA

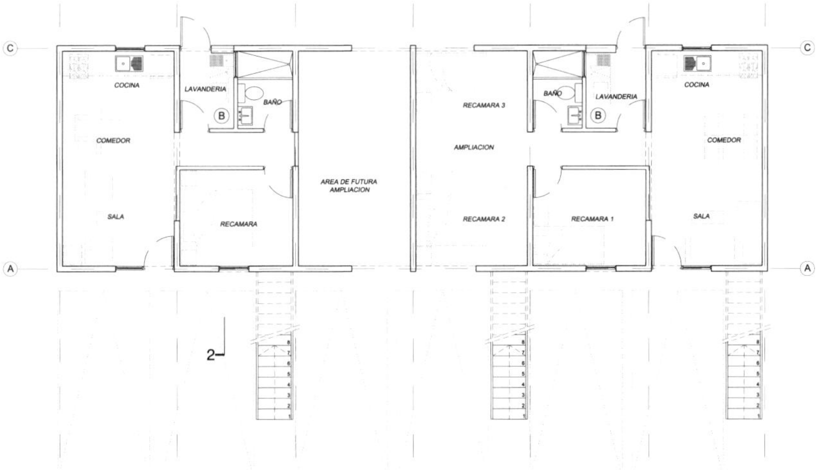
COCINA
LAVANDERIA
BAÑO
COMEDOR
SALA
RECAMARA
AREA DE FUTURA AMPLIACION
RECAMARA 3
AMPLIACION
RECAMARA 2
RECAMARA 1

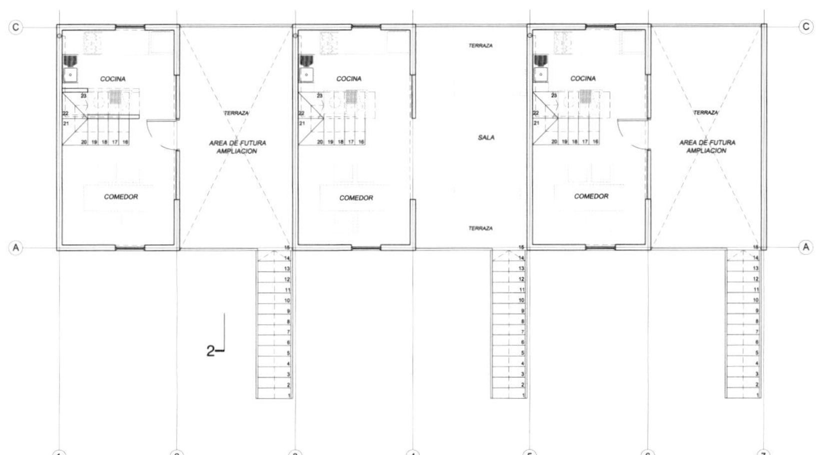
COCINA
COMEDOR
TERRAZA
AREA DE FUTURA AMPLIACION
SALA

Antofagasta, Chile

In order to make an efficient use of the sloping site that did not conflict with the given restrictions, Elemental situated the 95 units in strips parallel to the contours of the slope, the water line and the Circunvalación Avenue. The compound organization consists of two rows of houses on two terraces with seven to ten meters of difference in height. The housing unit is defined by structural three floor high partition walls. All complex items – firewall, facilities, circulation, and structure – are connected to this wall. This system generates a triple height interior void, in which families can make spatial modifications.

First stage of the new housing typology before expanding.

Left: The condition of the original housing in Antofagasta.
Right: Example of housing typologies developing in the market at the time.

Design/Construction Period: 2004-2009
Units: 95 House Complex
Initial House: 37.5 m²
Expanded House: 73.18 m²

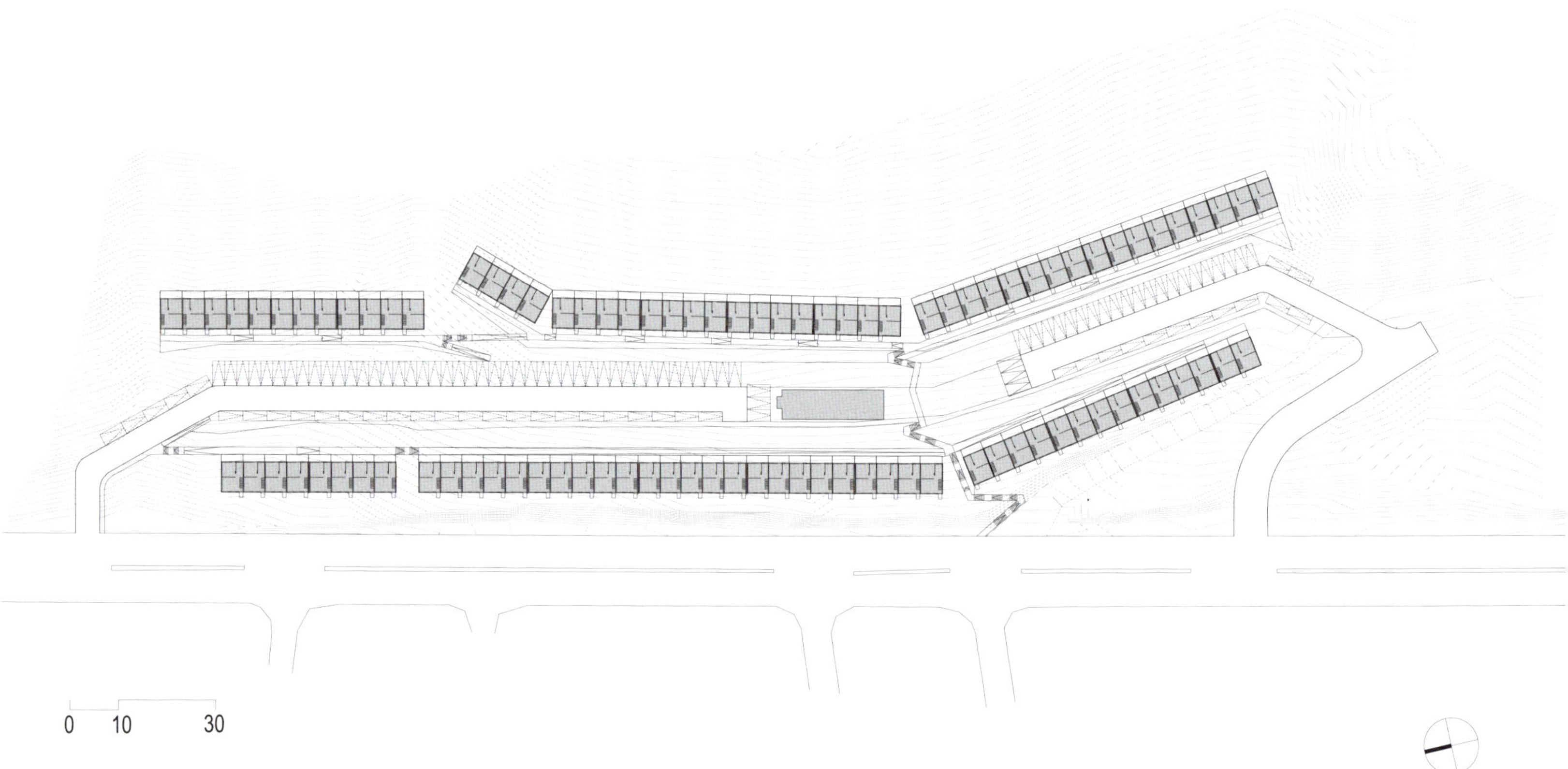
0 10 30

Service nucleus that predetermines the urban space, providing a regular frame for self-construction and augmenting the structure available for individual expansions making more efficient use of the lot and permitting higher densities without overcrowding.

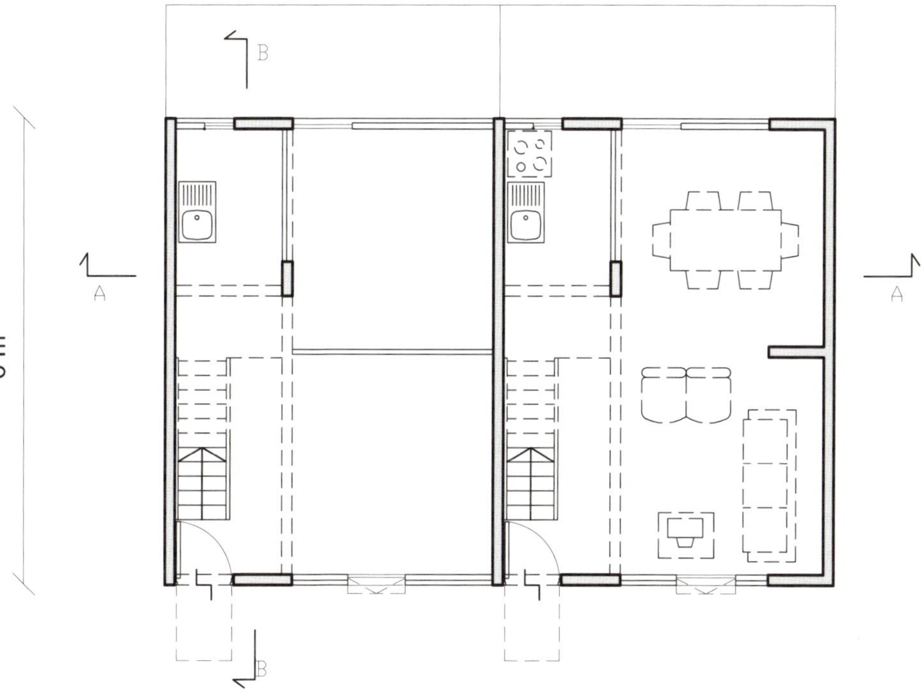

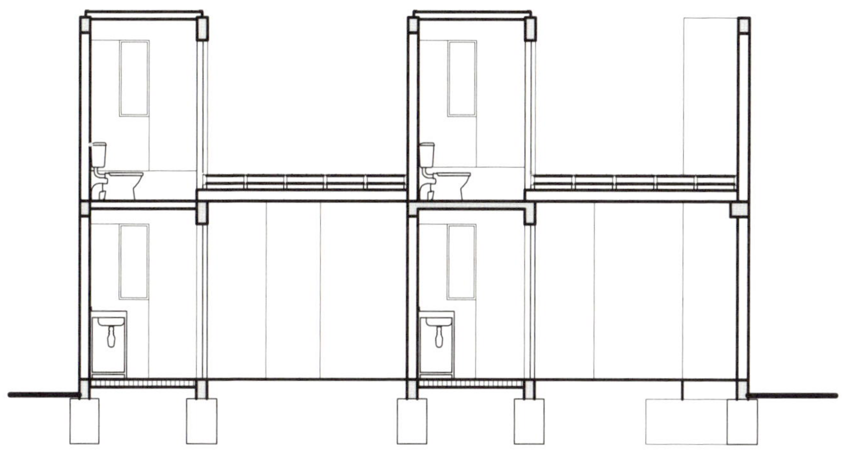

Renca
Santiago, Chile

The aim was to accommodate 170 families in a two-hectare site that used to be a clay quarry and was then used as a debris dump. Families lived across the street so it was desirable to maintain the location. But the cost of improving the soil was beyond the standard of what social housing could afford. Elemental developed a dense urban layout where all the units still had their own courtyard. Given that it rains in Santiago, the houses needed a waterproof exterior skin. Expansion was then expected to take place inside, in the triple height void of the unit.

The original condition of the community.

The three story housing was the typical typology in the market, bu was rejected by the community due to bad experience from simila housing areas.

Design/Construction Period: 2004-2008
Units: 170 House Complex
Initial House: 35 m²
Expanded House: 67 m²

124
125

ELEVACION FRONTAL

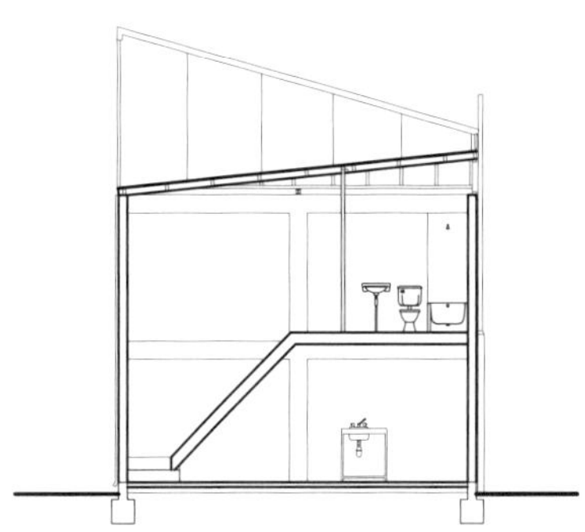

corte transversal

CORTE LONGITUDINAL

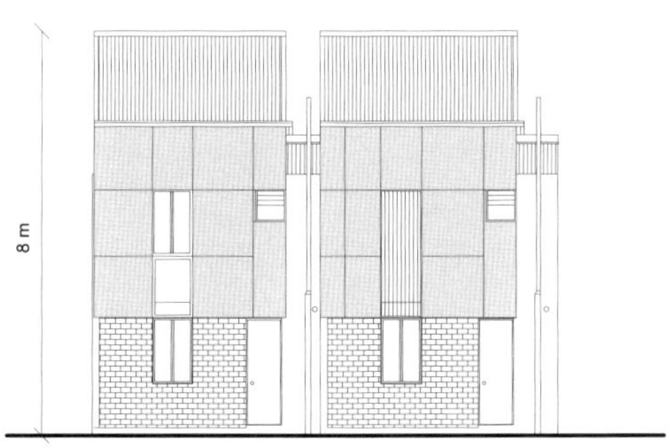

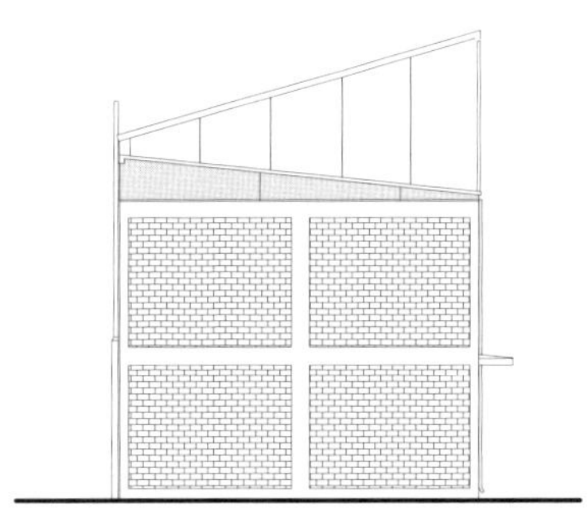

FACHADA POSTERIOR

The participatory process encouraging inhabitants to draw and fold their own future house in paper.

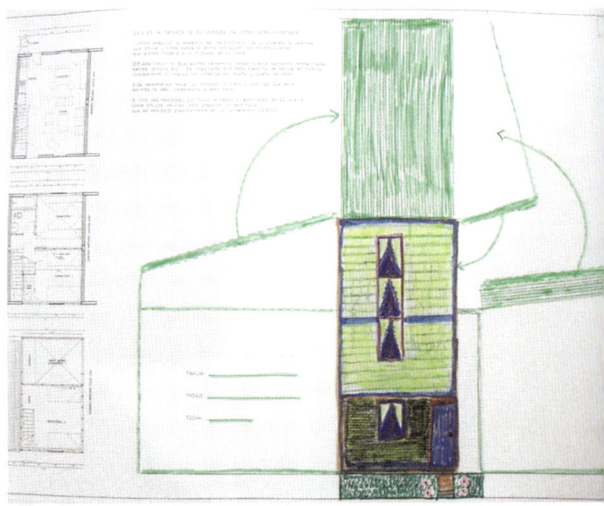

FLETE

Barnechea I-II
Santiago, Chile

This project is located in the most expensive neighborhood of Santiago. Elemental wanted, with very low budget subsidies, to allow the families to keep benefiting from the proximity to jobs, education, transportation, health facilities, recreation and public space. Units are arranged around a collective courtyard, a degree of closeness that is somewhere in between the private and the public space, which is crucial in fragile social environments. Starting from 150 units in the first phase, for a total of 1,000 families, Elemental continued toward a solution for a total of 363 families. Each inner wall was placed at a distance of three meters from each other, providing enough width for the living spaces. Expansion was expected to happen internally by building the floors between the available steel beams. The variation introduced was a pitched roof, reducing the dimension of the facade to two floors only, while conserving three interior floors. Costs were reduced by limiting the amount of structure and expensive finishes. The houses are organised as a sequence of only twelve units with a community courtyard at its center. Smaller communities reinforce the social networks and ensure proper maintenance.

Top: The original condition of the community.
Bottom: Housing typology available in the market.

Design/Construction Period: 2007-2010 and 2010-2014
Units: 150 + 213 House Complex
Initial House: 45 m²
Expanded House: 70 m²

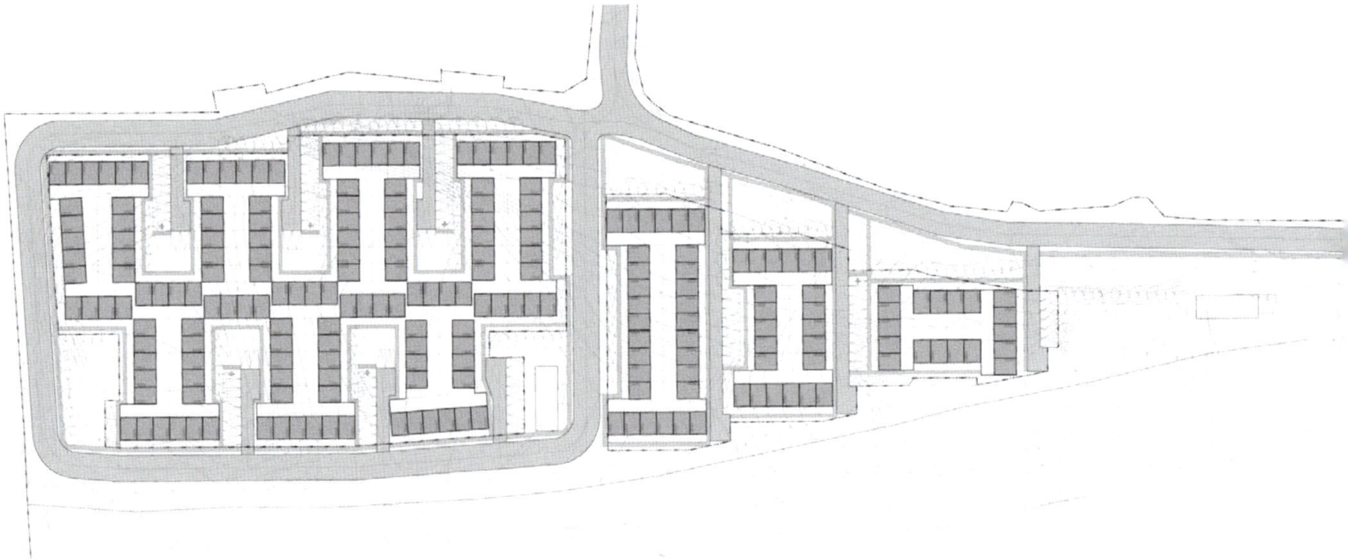

129

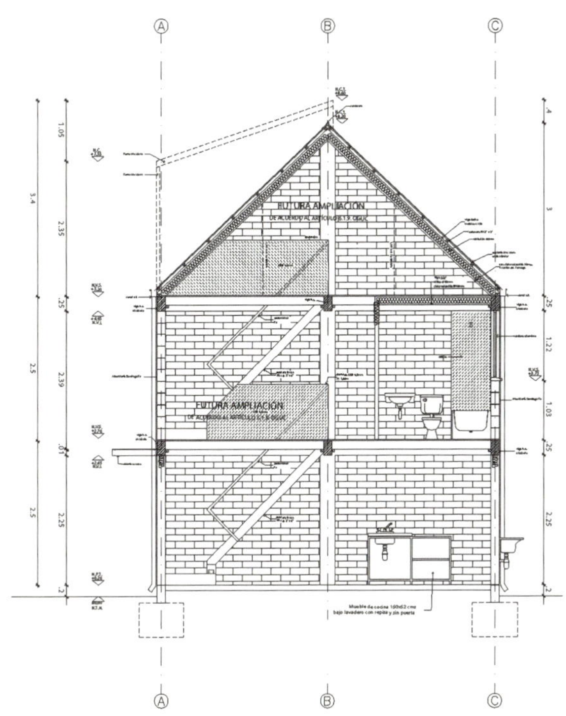
A
B
C
FUTURA AMPLIACIÓN
DE ACUERDO AL ARTÍCULO 6.1.9. OGUC
FUTURA AMPLIACIÓN
Mueble de cocina 100x52 cms
bajo lavadero con repisa y sin puerta
1.05
2.35
.25
2.39
.01
2.25
.2
3.4
2.5
2.5
.4
3
.25
1.22
1.03
.25
2.25
.2

(56-2) 25565050
ImprentaChile.cl

Villa Verde
Constitución, Chile

Initially, the city of Constitución had a housing deficit of around 3,00[illegible] homes, to which were added the homes destroyed and damaged b[illegible] the earthquake and tsunami in 2010.

The forestry company Celulosa Arauco y Constitución asked Elemental to develop a plan to support their employees and contractors so they could have access to home ownership, in the context of Chilean housing policies. This allowed Elemental to work for the first time with the high end of housing policy. Given the greater availability of resources, instead of taking one of their cheaper housing units and delivering it more finished, Elemental applied the principle of incrementality, but with an initial and final growth scenario of a higher standard: from an initial area of 57 m^2 each unit can grow to 85 m^2.

Design / Construction Period: 2010-2014
Land: 41,000 m^2 (484 house complex)
Initial House: 57 m^2
Expanded House: 85 m^2

The layout of collective spaces for around 20 families (units).

1st Floor Initial

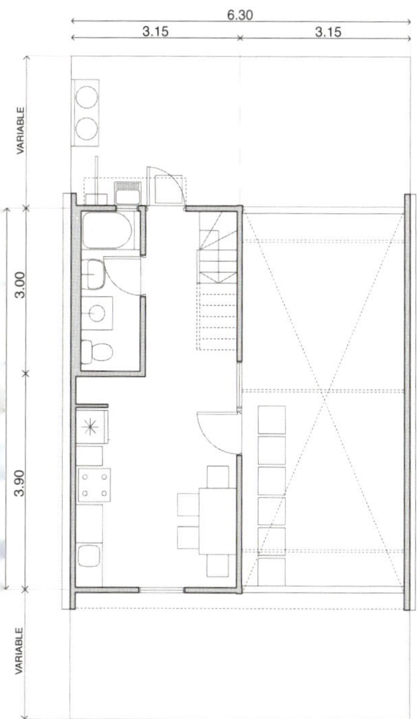

1st Floor expanded

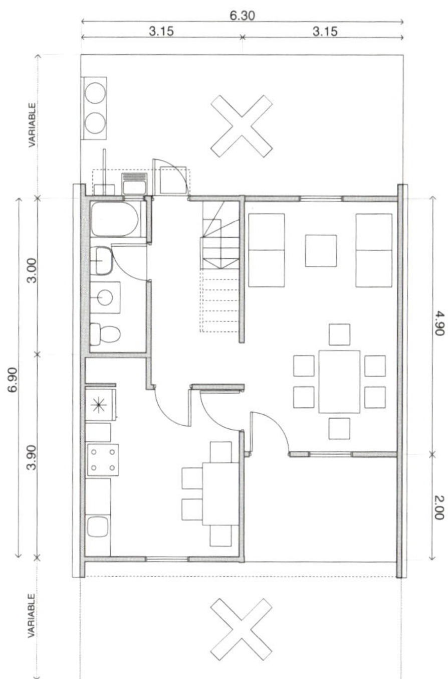

2nd Floor Initial

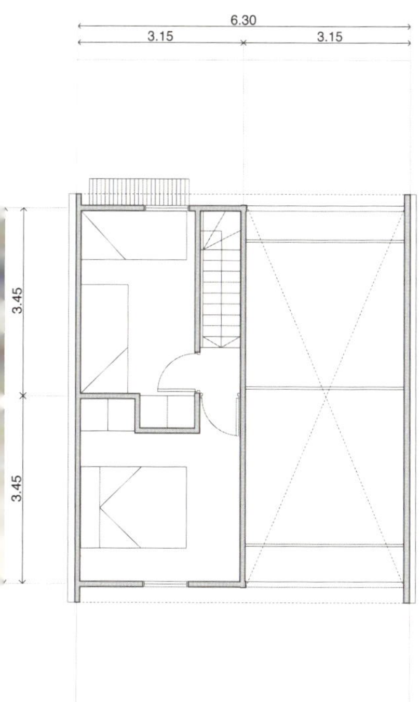

2nd Floor expanded

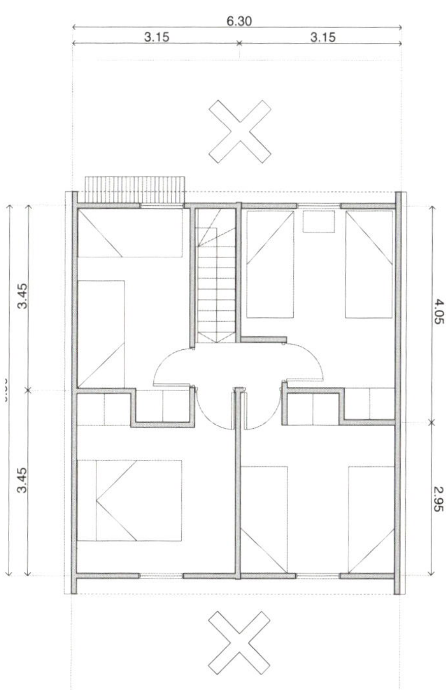

Vitra Children's Workshop
Weil am Rhein
Germany

The guiding principle behind the Vitra Children's Workshop was to make a building that was as natural and statement-free as a stone in nature. Vitra wanted a building that expressed flexibility, honesty and optimism, as well as leaving a low CO2 footprint. This was the framework guiding the building before the design process even began. Here Elemental used the traditional, double-pitched thatched roofs and construction methods of the local area as inspiration. In response to the request for a simple sustainable building, at the same time as wanting Zaha Hadid's Vitra Fire Station to be visible from the road, Elemental decided to keep the pre-exiting 400 m² cellar, and it was the shape of this cellar that determined the shape of the building above it. Instead of building new walls between the sloping thatched roof and the cellar, they based the project on what was already in situ, planning an entrance and inlets for natural light by removing more earth. Due to the financial crisis of 2008 the project was never realised, but it remains a prime example of Elemental's minimalist interventions and site-specific approach.

Vitra Children's Workshop
Project: 2008
Built Area: 600 m²

The thatched roof is the building, providing yet another visual icon for Vitra Campus.

Total plan of Vitra Campus, 2008. The three projects marked in red were developed simultaneously: Elemental's Vitra Children's Workshop, SANAA's Vitra Factory Building, and Herzog & de Meuron's VitraHaus.

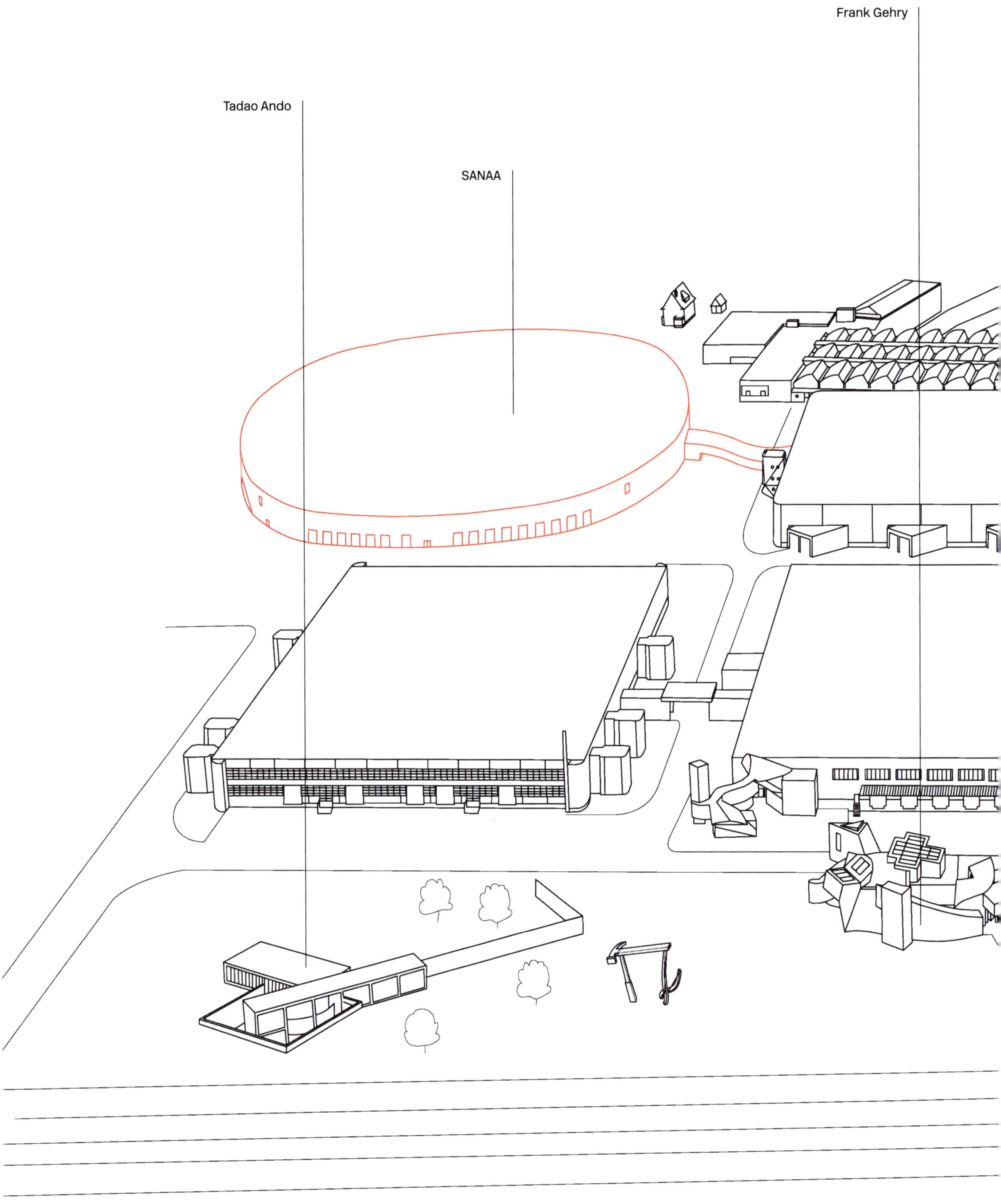

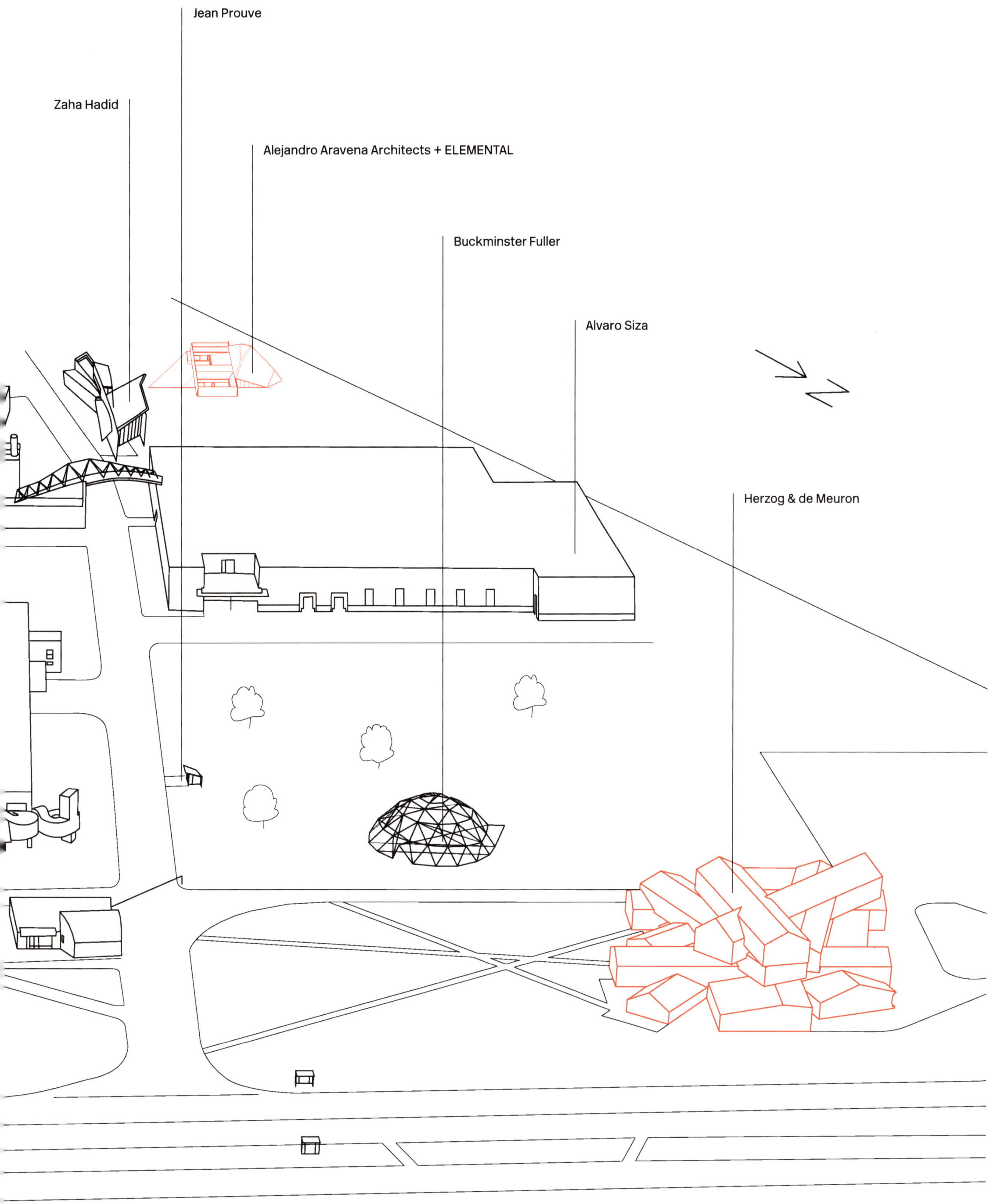
Jean Prouve
Zaha Hadid
Alejandro Aravena Architects + ELEMENTAL
Buckminster Fuller
Alvaro Siza
Herzog & de Meuron

The model shows the three parts of the building: the existing construction, the existing basement, and the new roof bringing everything together in a new structure.

Museum of Modern Art Medellín, Colombia

Architecture must accommodate the surrounding urban life, but a museum always faces a paradox: On the one hand, the museum by nature should be an open and accessible building, linked to its urban environment. On the other hand, the nature of its own program tends to produce hermetic buildings, with access control, security, and light limitations. Most museums situated in urban areas appear with rather blind walls leaving a large dead perimeter. Elemental propose to raise the airtight volume of the exhibition halls on a low-rise plinth which defines the private sphere of the museum. The ring that houses the rooms, floats on this plinth, freeing the horizon so that the view crosses the entire complex, taking into account the surrounding workshops and the park. A museum inevitably has to deal with two challenges: Light and the continuity of the exposure route. The circle being the geometric figure covering the largest area with the smallest perimeter, the exposure circuit with the shortest distance covers the greatest amount of exposure surface. The clear and unambiguous circulation through the circular space of the gallery housing the permanent and temporary art works alternate with transversal routes through the bridges, which in turn house the experimental art works. Since the galleries are all on one level, overhead light is always an option. By functioning as a reflection screen along the perimeter the double curved white wall makes it possible to modulate the inflow of the light, compensated with a second central light source from the heart of the ring. Two materialities establish links with the neighbourhood: bricks, a noble, ancient and abundant material, almost natural of the place, and exposed concrete, which not only establishes a continuity with the existing building, but also creates a neutral background to the main element.

Medellín Museum of Modern Art
Competition Project: 2009-2010
Building Area: 4,300 m²

The sketch shows how a cylinder is twisted then indented in the middle to create a hyperboloid. This makes the brick construction – located in an earthquake zone – more resistant to horizontal impact.

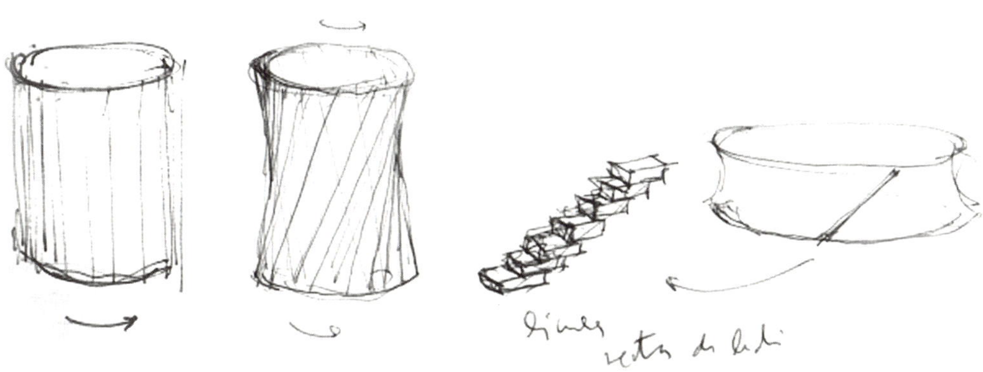

COCHOLGUE

A Geographical Problem Demands a Geographical Solution

PRES Constitución, 2010, Chile

On February 27th 2010 Chile was hit by an earthquake measuring 8.8 on the Richter scale, followed by a tsunami that mainly hit Constitución. Five hundred people lost their lives, and 300,000 homes were destroyed. Elemental were given just one hundred days to design everything in the city: public buildings, public spaces, housing, transport, energy supplies and – not least – to make Constitución tsunami-proof in the future. Such an essential master plan had to involve the people of the city. Elemental often describe their strategy with one sentence: "There's nothing worse than the right answer to the wrong question." Finding the right question is at the core of their work, and in this case it emerged that the design question that needed answering had far more layers than simply securing the city against future catastrophes. Constitución was a city that lacked public spaces and access to the sea. To meet these needs Elemental proposed creating a forest between the city and sea, arguing that a geographical problem demands a geographical solution. The next tsunami might first be in twenty years, so instead of making a barrier that could withstand it, the forest would provide the necessary protection at the same time as meeting the need for accessible public spaces which it would increase from 2.2 m² to 6.6 m² per inhabitant. Elemental's master plan also included immediate humanitarian relief with a strategy for water supplies and temporary housing. In the longer term the plan included a new cultural centre, a promenade on the coast that could be a tourist attraction and thereby help put the city back on its feet economically, as well as a new public piers for the local tradition of rowing.

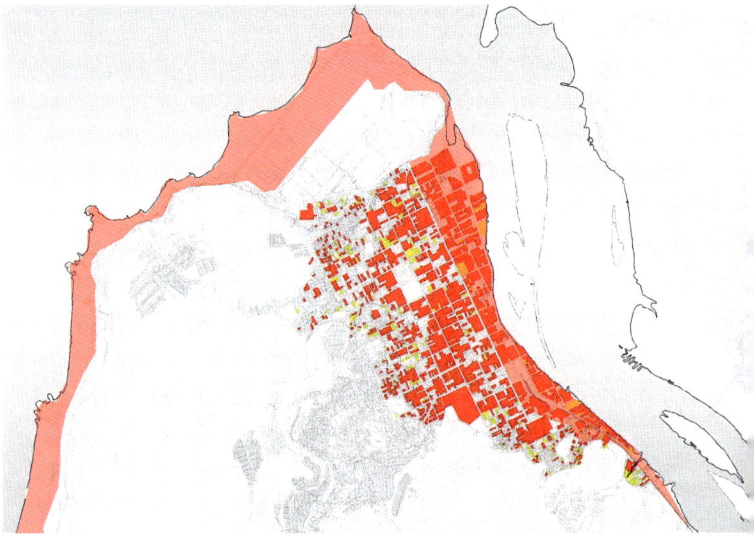

tsunami damage

earthquake damage

Design/Construction Period: 2010 – present
Building Area: 5,100,000 m² Masterplan

2009: Before the tsunami. 2010: After the tsunami. 2016: Under construction.
2025: Mitigation Park

New public spaces. Left: the forest between the ocean and the city. Below: the public piers.

PRES
CONSTITUCION

PRES
CONSTITUCION

Constitución Cultural Center was designed by Elemental as part of the reconstruction of Constitución. It is located on one side of the town square, inaugurating the new civic character of the public buildings of the city. The center includes independent and flexible spaces in order to give freedom of use to the community.

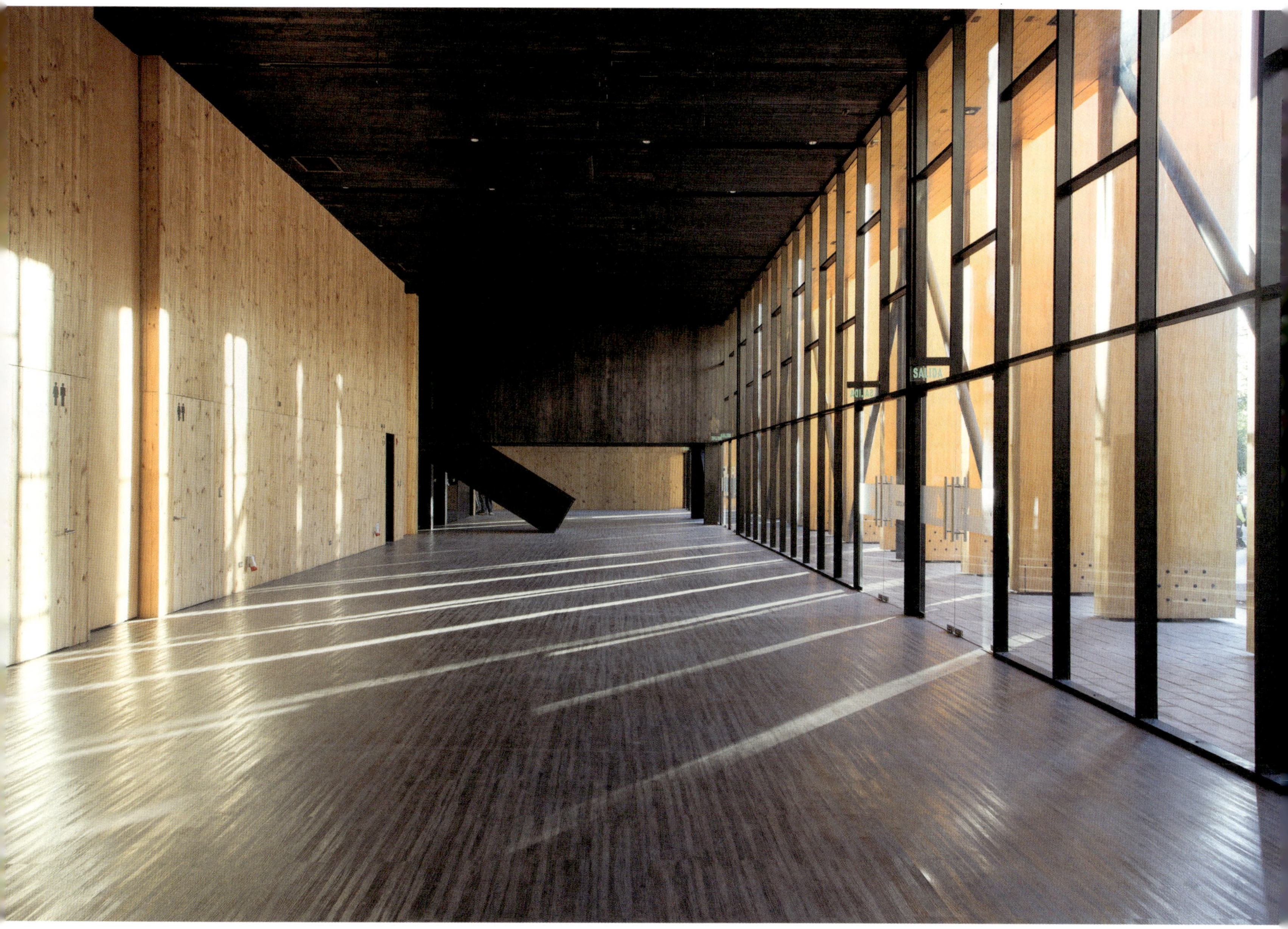

The Tourist Promenade and Cycle Lane consists of a series of coastal lookout points along the coast from Maule River's mouth to Maguellines Port in order to reinforce and highlight the natural heritage embodied by the huge rocks of this landscape. The platforms are connected by a 4.5 km cycle lane.

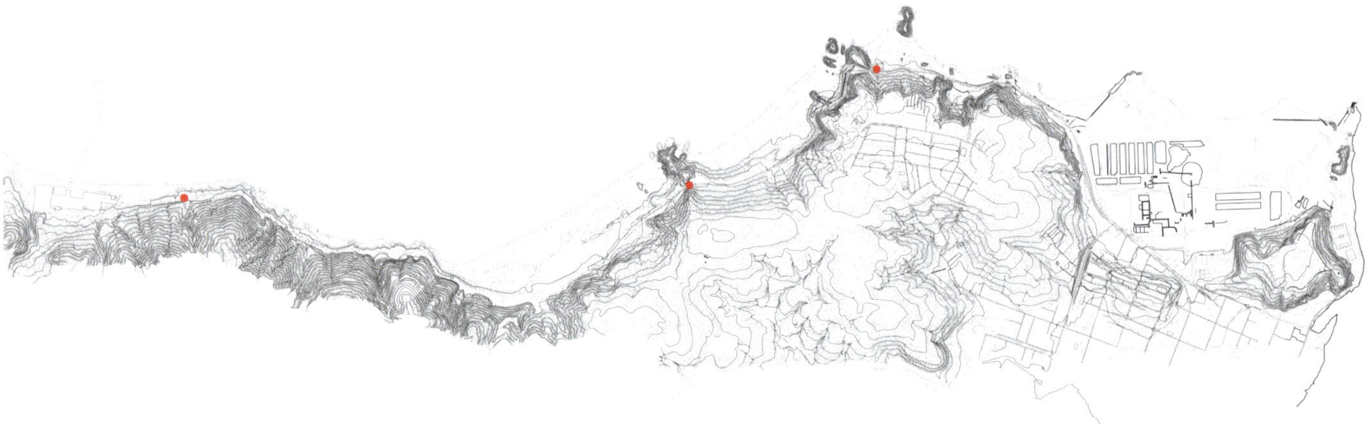

Balance, Equilibrium and Sustainability

Interview with Alejandro Aravena by Michael Juul Holm

MJH: For the exhibition at the Louisiana, you have designed this project that, as I see it, is all about equilibrium or balance, balancing forces. Some people will read it as metaphor. But I see it as strictly what it is – and also as a reference to some of your other projects. Could you try and clear up the mystery a little for the people that are about to see the exhibition?

AA: Well, first of all, I think it's important to agree that there's no metaphor in it. More than a metaphor, it's a visual statement, or a structural statement. At the same time, it will point to parts of the content of the exhibition. I guess it has to do with the different layers that the exhibition needs to have. The first-glance experience of the exhibition, when you enter the room and you see something, has to capture your interest. Then you start digging into different layers of the content. Those two installations work on that first idea of capturing our attention through this structural statement. Because they are interesting and beautiful in structure. But the space has some inherent content too, and we ask ourselves: What can we do here that is exceptional and unique to this space?

At the very core of our professional practice, there's an interest in connecting with the end user, or on the larger scale with society. One of the first books I wrote was called *Architectural Facts*. I may have expected people to interpret my work this or that way. But you can always go to facts. A shortcut, for example, is, in a given field, at the same time the shortest distance between point A and B and the longest possible view. There's no need for interpretation across a room. The diagonal of the room is at the same time the shortest way to go across it and the longest view. That's a fact. Can we start a project which, despite the cultural differences, connects to the audience through basic facts? Weight, gravity? We all inevitably feel the weight of things. And architecture, even in its most modest version, weighs quite a bit. Even a modest installation like the one we are doing at the Louisiana is a couple of tons. Whatever we want to say in an exhibition starts from something that can be shared as a physical experience. A ton weighs the same in Chile and ind Denmark. Can we create that common language with a common experience, not based on words but on facts, connected to the human perception? This has always been an interest of ours.

The more we can start an architectural process based on those facts and common experiences, the better are our chances to engage. And I guess that's the ultimate reason why we agree to do an exhibition. We don't want to be enigmatic, but to be as transparent as possible in sharing what we do. The cube in the main room is a question of weight and gravity – and you're right, it's not a metaphor. Anyone, even if you're not an expert, can see that here, in order for architecture to become real, you have to make matter fight gravity. You can make it more invisible or, as in this case, show it more. We felt it pertinent to let these forces be expressed in the exhibition.

And the installation is directly connected to the title *So far …*, which has this double meaning of retrospection and the fact that we come from so far away, from another hemisphere. Turning the horizontal to the vertical, left to right, in front to behind, we twist the axis to bring about a different understanding. Changing the axis of the exhibition from things on the wall, as in a horizontal view, to things that are either on top or below. At the very beginning, when we were first contacted by the curator, Kjeld Kjeldsen, our first reaction was to build the entire exhibition upside down. You would enter a world in reverse.

— That would be metaphor!

Yes. It would be a spectacle but not necessarily interesting. We went on to a second version, and a third version, until we found something that still communicated the change in the axis. We're lowering the horizon, so you enter the big installation almost crawling into the space. This is another fact: When you are lying on the ground, when you lie back on the ground and look up, something happens. I may be sitting on the ground and looking up, and it's not the same thing as lying down, putting your head on the ground – something happens. We wanted that experience of lying on the ground, flat, looking up into films that are showing our hemisphere from above. There's a fascination in looking at things from above. It gives a more objective view. In plan, you see buildings, open layers of projects. Again, we were trying to go back to some facts, and this had a formal translation. In order to know where the horizon is, let's have a weight that forces you to go underneath, lie flat on your back on the ground, feel your own weight against the ground. Something mysterious happens in these basic situations, and we always try to make different projects identify that basic irreducible moment when you find the relationship with your body in the space.

— You were working in 2016 as the curatorial director of the Architecture Biennale in Venice. What did you take with you as architects? How does it bring anything useful to architecture? Is it a professional circulation of ideas, or is it mostly spin and socializing?

There have certainly been exchanges – intellectual and creative – with some of the offices that participated in the Biennale. But you can't say that is a general thing. There are so many different ways of approaching architecture. From my point of view, the Biennale tries to explain in a simple way for common people what new solutions you can find in the world of architecture. We ask the architects to show their works through different layers: first a two-second impact, another ten seconds to read the captions, another minute to read the basic information. In exhibitions you have to find some way – without losing quality – to communicate with the masses. On another level, as architects, we learn a lot. Seeing different projects for us was incredible. I can't speak for all the participants, but for us it was incredible.

I don't know if the interaction in the world of architecture is working well enough. Often, the things that we find more interesting and nurturing, from which we intellectually swallow information, are not architectural shows, but derive from everyday discussions, like when we have lunch every day at the office. This is a moment when we don't necessarily talk about work. We talk about films, music, travels or whatever. We're very nerdy in that sense, we find pleasure in sharing nerd data about things. Often from science, from the social sciences quite a lot, and anthropological things. Evolution, the origin of mankind. When was fire 'invented'? A more cultural discussion but always based on knowledge.

What architectural shows normally share is that you're able to go back home and, in very simple terms, explain to others what moved you, what you discovered. And you're able to tell a story: Have you ever heard about this and that? Yes, we have always thought that the paradigm was A, B, and C. But there's new evidence now that has proven that the paradigm has shifted. In three sentences, you have created the bridge, established a first connection, and created the surprise of a new thing. Normally, that doesn't happen at architectural or art shows, which can be very cryptic, very hermetic. Nobody knows what the point is. To have a point is banal, because it's not mysterious enough.

In Venice we deliberately invited practices in keeping with the title of the exhibition, *Reporting From the Front*. The first thing is to identify the problem, and we asked each of them: What is your front? Is it inequalities? War? Vanity? The environment? Garbage? It doesn't have to be a humanitarian thing. It could be: Look, this is a greedy, shitty developer's world where I have to deliver housing for the middle class and nobody wants to give me a millimeter to produce quality. That's also a front. Producing quality in the real estate market is very hard.

In a very simple way, let's identify the question or the problem. Second: What is your contribution? We asked each participant to send us a handwritten sheet of A4 paper to hang in the first room. Share your problem with us and say what you have done about it. If you can't explain it in very simple terms, maybe it's because you don't have a point. Then the question was either dismissed or re-asked. That was our strategy. That was one of the things that, for us, was so fascinating. We were entering one project after the other. Having this stone vault by Ochsendorf and Block without any glue, any connector! Just gravity working, avoiding bending, to save 70% of the matter of a structure. The consequences for the environment! It hit you in the face. In the next room somebody is working with bamboo, with a material that is renewable, that will change the laws in a given country. A feast of intellectual dishes or, in this case, emotional dishes one after the other, that nurtured your intellect. I guess once more we didn't know this had to be the strategy. But at least for us, it proved to be such a rewarding professional experience.

We wanted to make sure this Biennale was not an expression of cynicism or skepticism. You know, like: "The world is doomed. Nothing to do. So why should I give a shit about it?" Nor a hippie thing: "Let's go and change the world." It was neither the NGO nor the market approach. Somewhere in between: a lot of practicalities and constraints and optimism. That was our feeling too for our own practice. If a guy in South Africa with almost no resources is able to change a situation that is very complex – crime, violence, insecurity, racism – then there's no excuse for me, in a much more comfortable environment, not to make a change too. If a guy in Colombia with drug cartels and the worst *sicarios* walking around was able to change things, and the quality of the politicians was able to change the city, there's no excuse for me not to change things too. It was not romantic dreaming about a better world, but a number of examples of actual practical work being done all over the world.

Another attitude that lies staggeringly close in these times, especially if you are not very critical about the media interpretations of the state of things, is "Look, there's nothing to do anyway. I am just going to show beautiful objects to look as if I'm doing something." But that's just decoration. We were asking the exhibitors to share the complications and the problems. We knew some of the stories, and sometimes in the Biennale they want to make a very clean, polite presentation. But we were saying: No, share all the difficulties you had to go through: the corruption, the unwillingness of the authorities, or even people bullying you. We preferred power over perfection in the projects that we were asking to be shown there. We were not interested in the clean outcome. To have done something in Medellín is so powerful. The sense of perfection that the general public is also expecting from architecture: Well, sometimes it's not possible, and that's okay. Having to choose our preference was putting power above perfection.

— Coming back to the show here at the Louisiana – did you take the Venice experience with you into these galleries?

Yes and no. One of the things we brought here from the Biennale is that the way you acquire knowledge in exhibitions is through emotions. We want to share knowledge, we want to communicate the way you operate. The way to achieve that could be intellectual, could be technical, could be experiential, but in an exhibition, the way it enters into your system is through emotion. We have certainly learned about reactions from the guests and how to meet them. But our installations in this show are not linked directly to any of our earlier projects, not as metaphor or as an echo. It's one more project. It's another thing. It has to do with the fact that you cannot move architecture to an exhibition. You just see pictures, plans, renderings or models. You cannot really experience architecture in an architectural exhibition. So why shouldn't we create or treat the exhibition as a project in itself, so that at least in a certain dimension you can experience something that *is* architecture. That's why we have these site-specific installations.

It has to do with the way you experience architecture, not only the sight or sound, but also the body: where you are sitting, lying; whether it's tall, high, hot or cold – these are some of the dimensions that we're trying to work into the installations.

Nowadays almost everything is already on the Internet. In principle you don't go to an exhibition to be informed of something that you had no idea of before. It's already out there. The only thing that we thought made sense is that you share something that under normal circumstances doesn't make it to the Internet. The internal cooking of things, the notion of the original – you go there and the sketchbooks are going to be the actual sketchbooks. If we couldn't do something that had a physical presence and the value of the original, then we wouldn't even want to make an exhibition.

— You had a prize for the sustainability of your work. What is sustainability to you?

In one sentence: It's the rigorous use of common sense. For example, we're designing a project for a company in Portugal, EDP – Energias de Portugal – for their headquarters in Lisbon. And then it's not wanting to do anything until we understand the context and the applicable laws and regulations. In the center of Lisbon, there are a lot of regulations about the historic site and the neighbors. It is a question of reclaimed landfills: how much you can dig – or not. Questions of humidity, salt, air, wind. Heat in the summer, temperature variation. Pollution. Birds, probably! So we approach the building with all that in mind. To tackle these issues we considered the orientation, direct sun radiation, thermal mass, and maintenance over time. And we did that by just following what we thought was pertinent using common sense. We submitted it to a company that deals with the whole process and it came out as LEED gold. We didn't go for that at the first place, we took care of all the other stuff and ended up classified as sustainable. The only thing we did was to be very rigorous in the use of common sense; defining the materials, the orientation and so on. Then you come out of the thing with LEED gold. I guess that would be good – if we were all rigorous in postponing wanting something until we can transform what is pertinent into something that is even aesthetically expressive!

Of course, we want the building to be a contribution to the historical neighborhood and to add something positive to it. You have incredible masterpieces around, so it's not as if you can do whatever you like. We were ourselves surprised, as was the company that received the project. They said, this is the first time we've done a project like this, and without any discussion of it, we've gone directly to LEED gold – even on a low budget. In the end, sustainability is the outcome of a process that uses common sense in defining the directions for sustainability. It's not a preconceived goal. Which is where I think most people struggle with trying to be sustainable: How are we to be sustainable, are we talking about the local environment, recirculation of energy, materials or economical sustainability? I guess the notion of sustainability has become more complex now. It's not just an environmental sustainability. It's economic. It's a political, social sustainability. I guess it has become more challenging.

If we follow this approach of postponing – not eternally, but at least for a couple of weeks not wanting to want anything – then, once we've dealt with the questions, we can jump into the void and make a proposal. And from that moment on, we organize conversations around a proposal, not a diagnosis. This is not the work of a consultant. This is the work of an author that takes the risk of proposing something. And this is the biggest difference between a consultancy and an authorship. A consultant provides all the information so that the client can take a decision. As an author, you collect information and you take the decision and offer it to the client. If you just try to apply what has already worked for you once, I guess the chances of failure are high, particularly as the questions are becoming more and more difficult. So maybe the 'sustainability' outcome is the same. But it may not be economically, politically or socially sustainable. And that's why we just have to make sure that we have enough time, at least, for these questions. We will keep a bubble of intimacy and wait carefully for the moment when the question has been formulated and then, in the most honest – and hopefully creative – way, we jump into the void of making a proposal. The number of projects we can take on is limited. We have chosen not to grow, for example. It is done within a certain number of people, so it's a group, a certain culture that we want to keep. And in the end, that, I guess, is what keeps us creatively alive. We feel enthusiastic about this approach, but it requires you to be careful and rigorous in not doing everything all over again all the time. Maybe there are people that have the talent for having one idea after the other in one day or so. That isn't the case with us. For us, it doesn't take forever, but it's also not that fast.

Ocean Winery
Nierstein, Germany

The best wine is made by allowing nature to take its course with as little human interference as possible. The architecture of the winery is therefore designed to support the transformation of grapes into wine, from crushing the grapes underfoot, to sedimentation and fermentation, then bottling and ageing. If the tannic acid in wine to remain intact, pumping wine upwards before bottling is to be avoided. Here gravity, as the force that moves the grapes through the process, is the most important element of winemaking. Ocean Winery is therefore located on the most optimal slopes close to the terroirs. There is a tower for wine tasting and sales, a block resting on the slope housing production, and a horizontal platform supporting the other building elements that functions as a courtyard where the grapes are delivered. The project was a turning point for Elemental's architectural language and methodology, cutting back on all superfluous design to work solely with elements relevant to the function of the building. "We went from designing geometrical forms with lots of edges, to creating forms with no more than four sides. The value lies in the way they relate and connect to each other, rather than the individual design of each element. The shift came from wanting to create architecture capable of standing the test of time, cutting back on the unnecessary, and following forces that are larger than life. Like shortcuts. Or gravity."

Ocean Winery
Project: 2009
Building Area: 4,200 m²

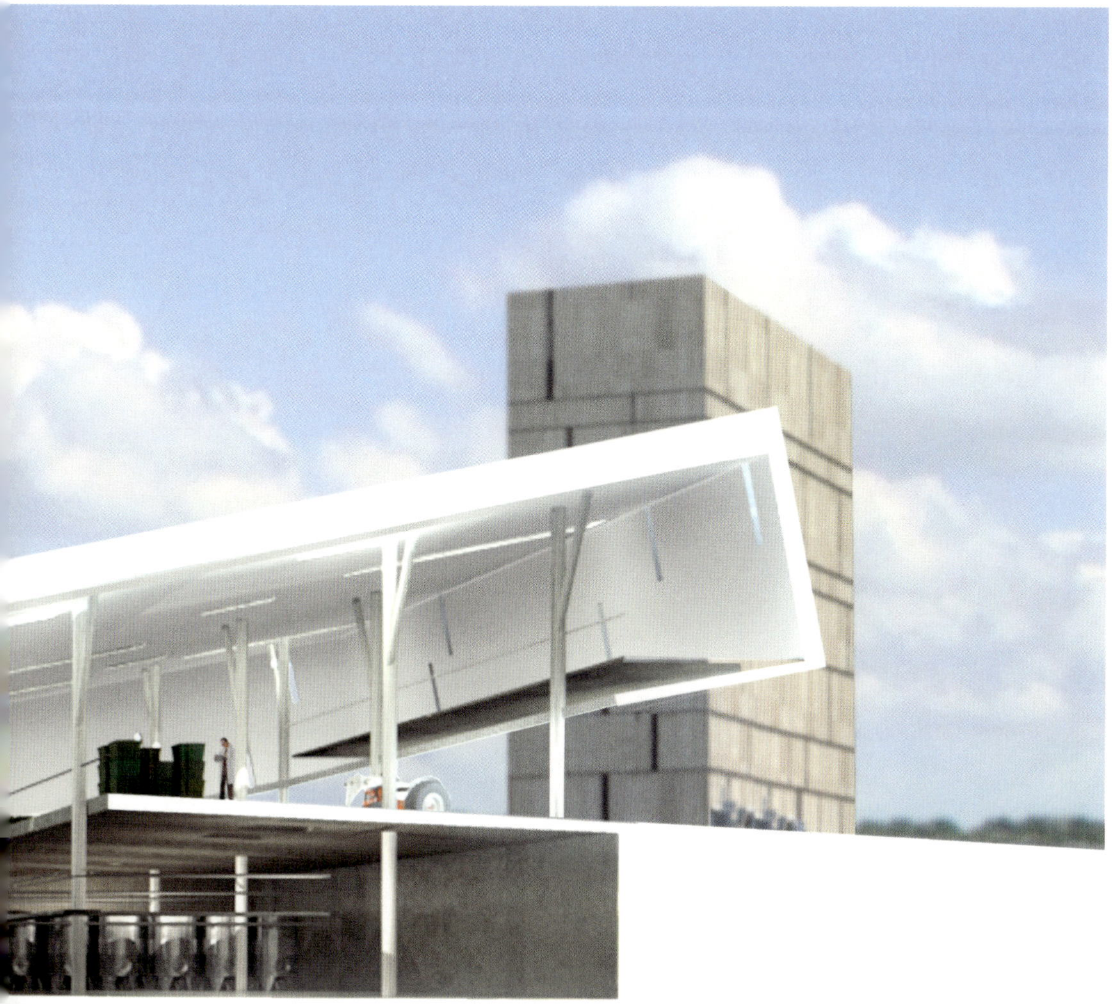

Sectional view of the production facilities with different stages of production on descending plateaus on the hillside.

Ochoquebradas House
Los Viloa, Chile

Ochoquebradas – eight gorges – is a private developer's commission of designs for 16 weekend homes by sixteen Japanese and Chilean architects. The nature here is brutal and the Pacific far from peaceful, meeting the coast in a torrent of white foam. Both the location and remit offered the opportunity to explore the most elementary and primitive aspects of dwelling. The absence of an individual client with specific demands, and the fact that a holiday home is a second home, made it possible for Elemental to challenge conventional ideas of a modern house and focus on the most essential functions and needs. Elemental's house consists of three elements: the first is horizontal and houses the owner's private quarters; the second vertical element is for guests and has a roof terrace; the third rests on the first two and contains a fireplace. The fireplace represents the oldest, revolutionary advance for humankind, and together with the provision of shelter forms the basis of the first settlements in human history. The aim of creating a home with this level of primitiveness is expressed in three simple rectangular blocks, solely held together by gravity. The materials reflect the brutal nature surrounding them, and will age like stone but still be comfortable to live in. Five sides of the blocks are cast in poured concrete, and the last is constructed using the wood used to make the casting moulds for the concrete. The other invited architects were: O + H, Junya Ishigami, Atelier Bow Wow, Akihisa Hirata, Kazuyo Sejima, Kengo Kuma, Ryue Nishizawa, Sou Fujimoto, HLPS arquitectos, Cristian Undurraga, Felipe Assadi, Max Nuñes, WMR arquitectos, Izquierdo Lehmann and Guillermo Acuña.

Ochocquebradas House
Design/Construction Period: 2013-2015
Building Area: 289 m^2

Elemental's take on a holiday home celebrates the basic functions of a dwelling. The sketch focuses on the ambience of a secular, ceremonial space.

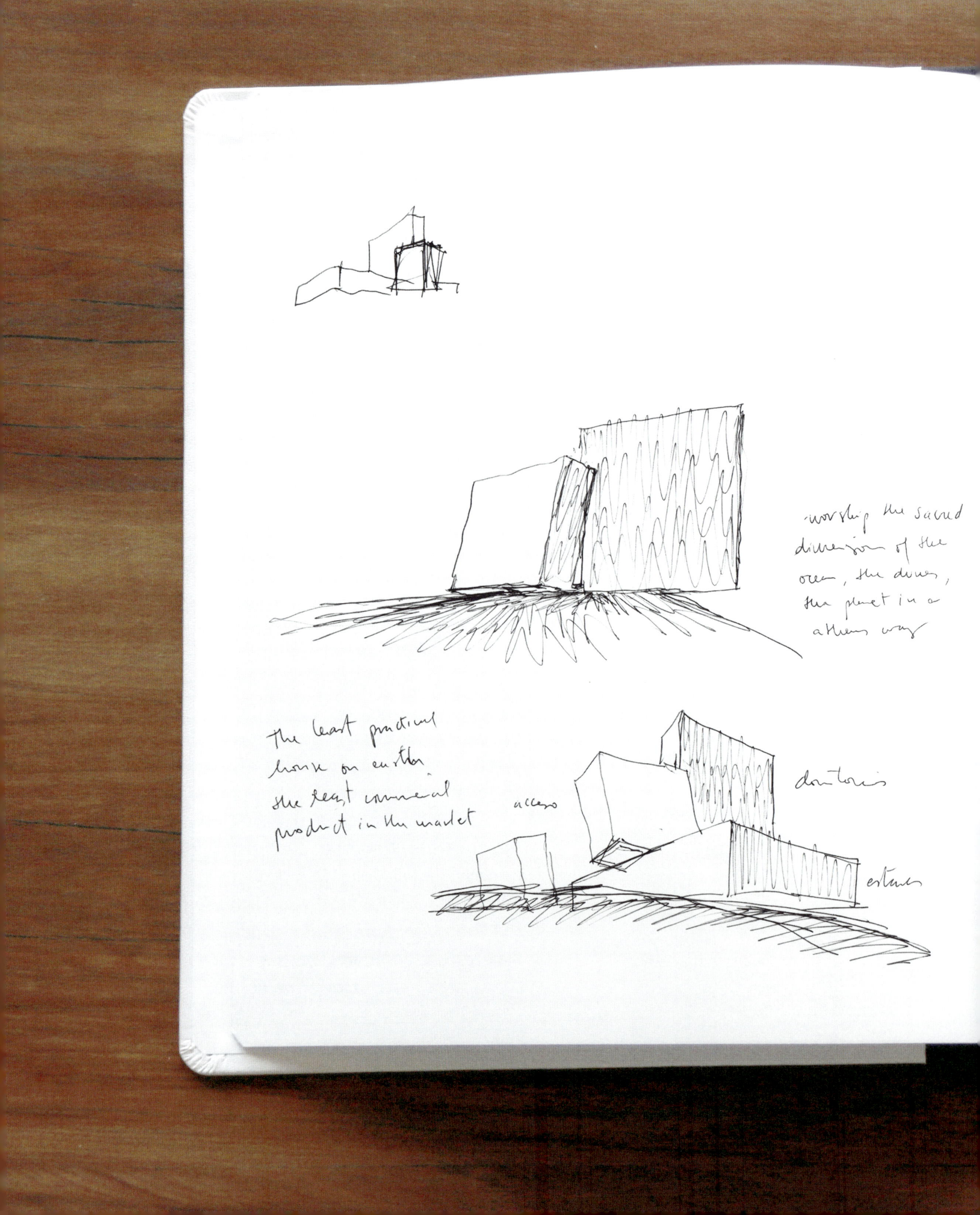

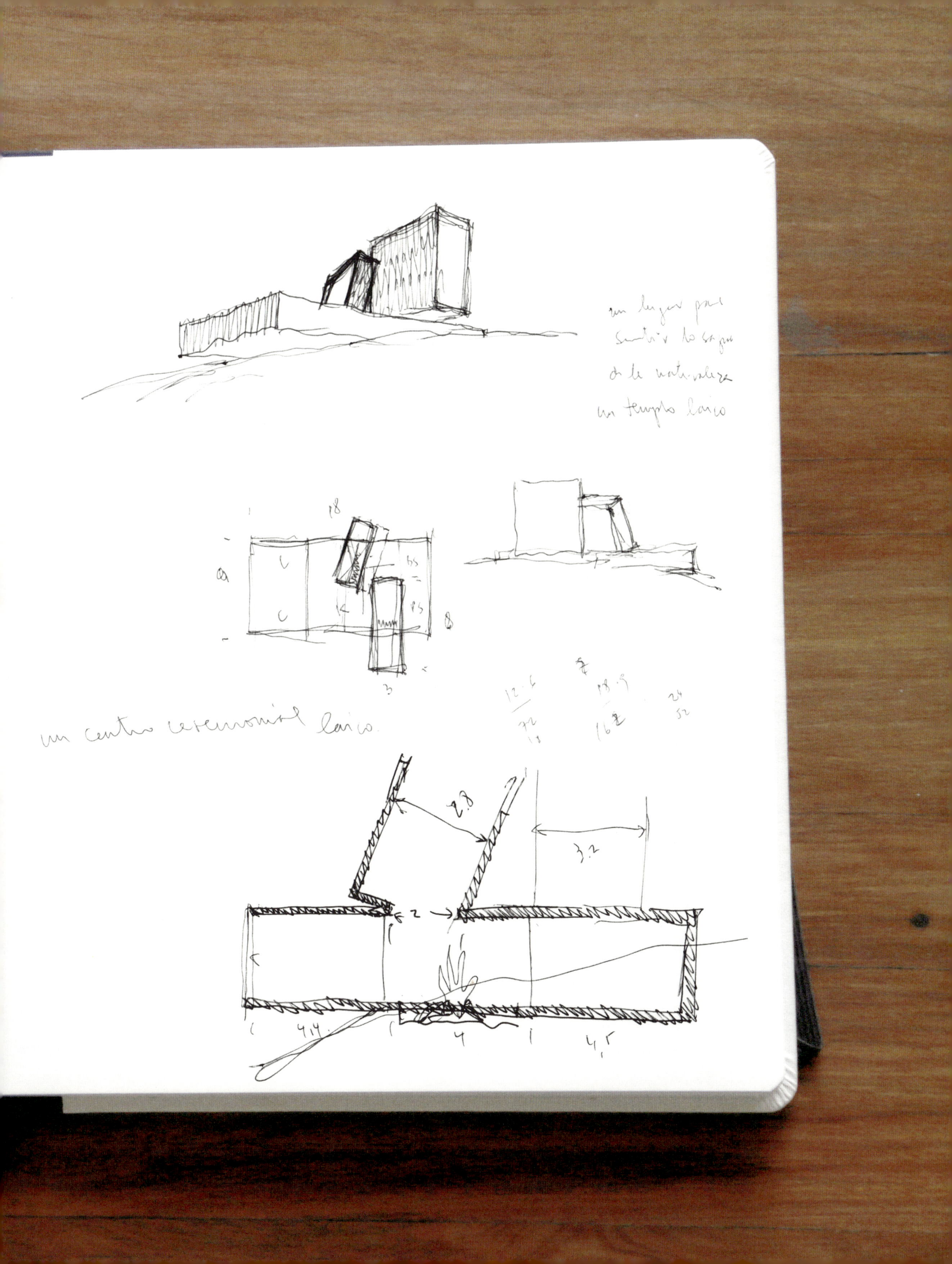
un templo laico
un centro ceremonial laico
2.8
3.2
4.4
4
4,5

Sectional view of the private part of the dwelling and the connection to the guest's quarters.

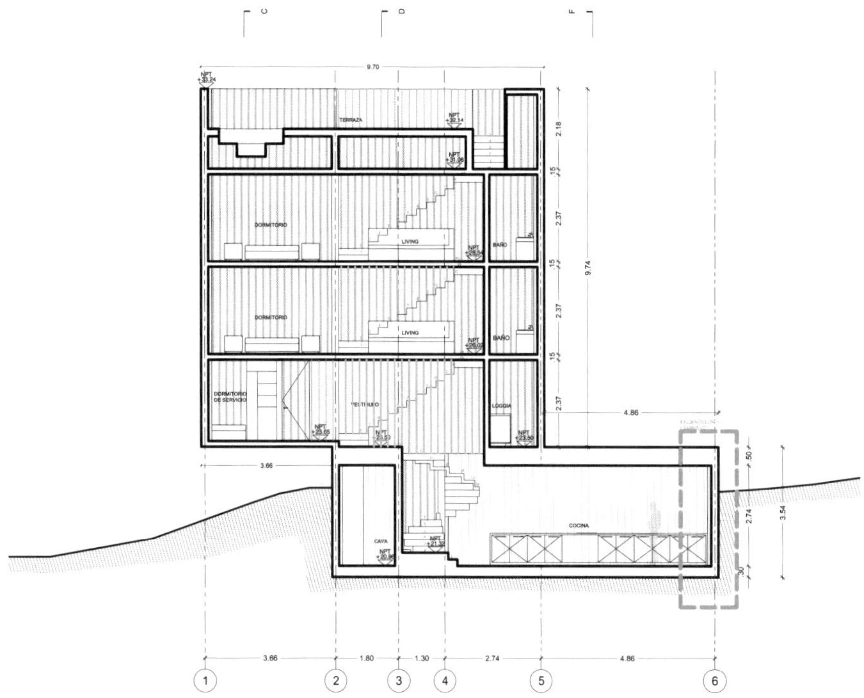

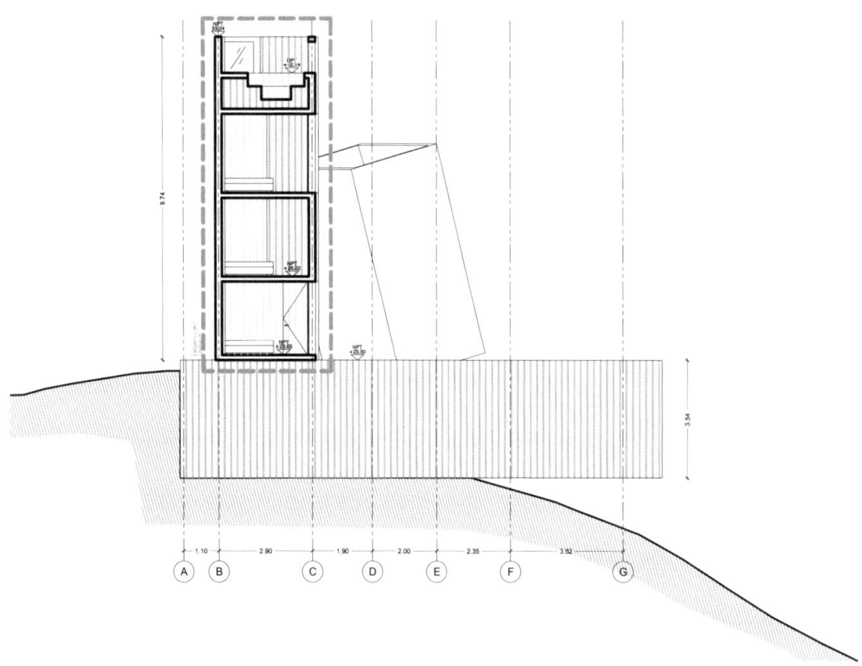

The fireplace is located in the horizontal block with a direct view of the ocean.

natural

dark = insecure 2

3

safe but unnatural

4

invisible when not in use

Energias de Portugal
Lisbon, Portugal

The project had to comply with a master plan retaining the existing public space from the hills to the river, which resulted in splitting the building's mass into two linear blocks whilst retaining the illusion of a single entity. The area of the public space is folded with a slight slope, connecting the two linear blocks below the apex. Being on the second row of Lisbon's urban grid, the view of the river had always been more theoretical than real, but this was resolved by the artificial slope: previously the building in front had blocked any view of the river, but the creation of an outlook point ramp resting on the slope created enough height to provide a view of the Tagus. To integrate energy efficiency with the character of the building, the public square was approached as a carved monolith to ensure sufficient thermal mass. At the same time the apparent erasure of floors within produced a sense of civic monumentality. By contrast, on the peripheral facades each floor is made explicit to bring a degree of domesticity to the offices. A deep grid of linear elements work as a brise soleil, deflecting direct sunlight to reduce heat and thereby energy consumption. Even though it wasn't a predefined goal, the building complies LEED gold certificate requirements for buildings that save energy, water and resources, at the same time as generating less waste and supporting human health.

Energias de Portugal
Design: 2017-2018 (ongoing)
Building Area: 3,800 m^2

What informs the form of the project? Sustainability and communal areas versus private offices, creating the space for different kinds of work processes and encounters.

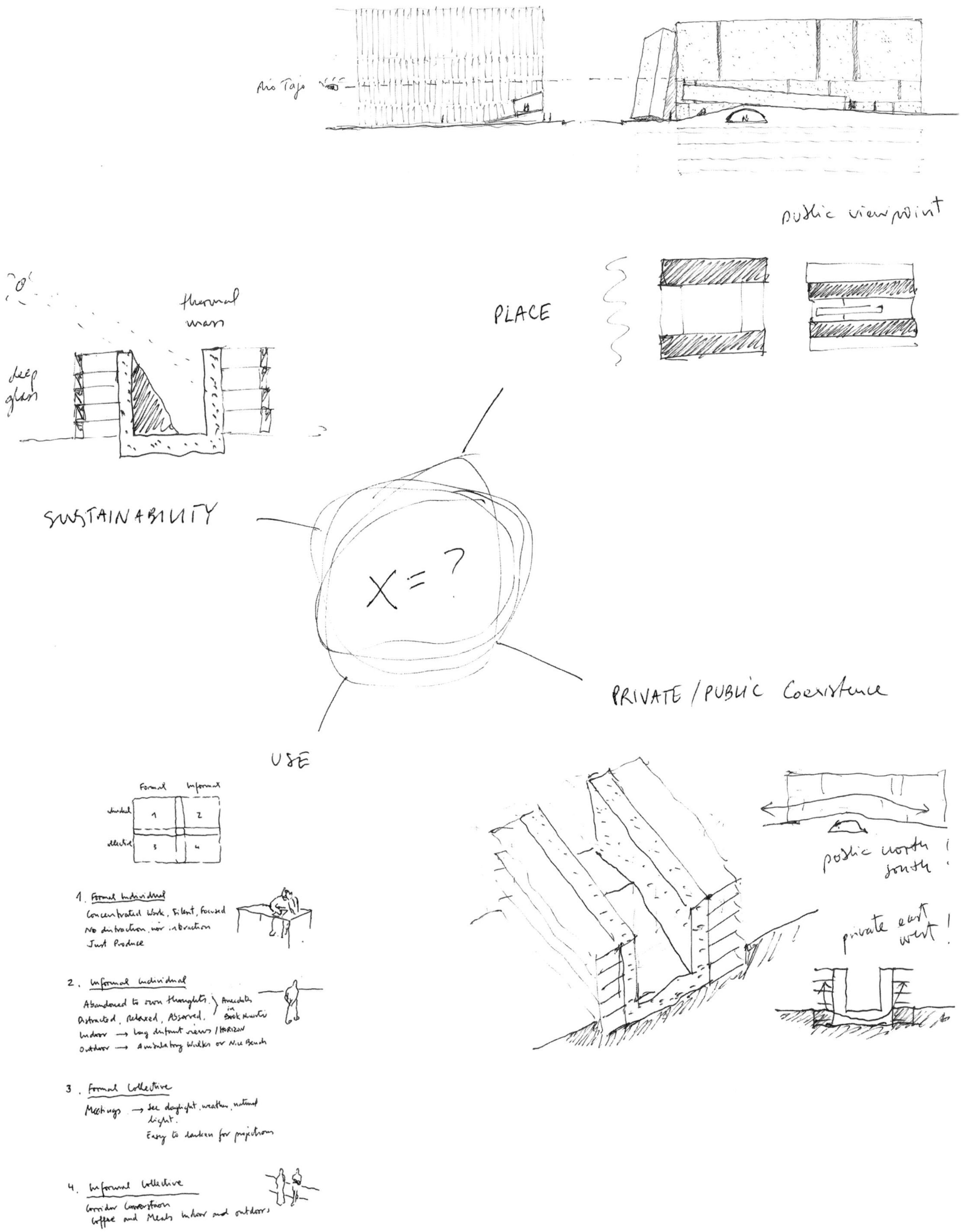

public viewpoint
thermal mass
deep glass
PLACE
SUSTAINABILITY
X = ?
PRIVATE / PUBLIC Coexistence
USE
Formal
Informal
1
2
3
4
1. Formal Individual
Concentrated Work, Silent, Focused
No distraction, nor interaction
Just Produce
2. Informal Individual
Abandoned to own thoughts.
Distracted, Relaxed, Absorved.
Indoor → Long distant views / HORIZON
Outdoor → Ambulatory Walks or Nice Bench
3. Formal Collective
Meetings → See daylight, weather, natural light.
Easy to darken for projections
4. Informal Collective
Corridor Conversation
Coffee and Meals indoor and outdoors
public north south
private east west

A narrow footbridge resting on the slope creates a visual connection to the Tajo.

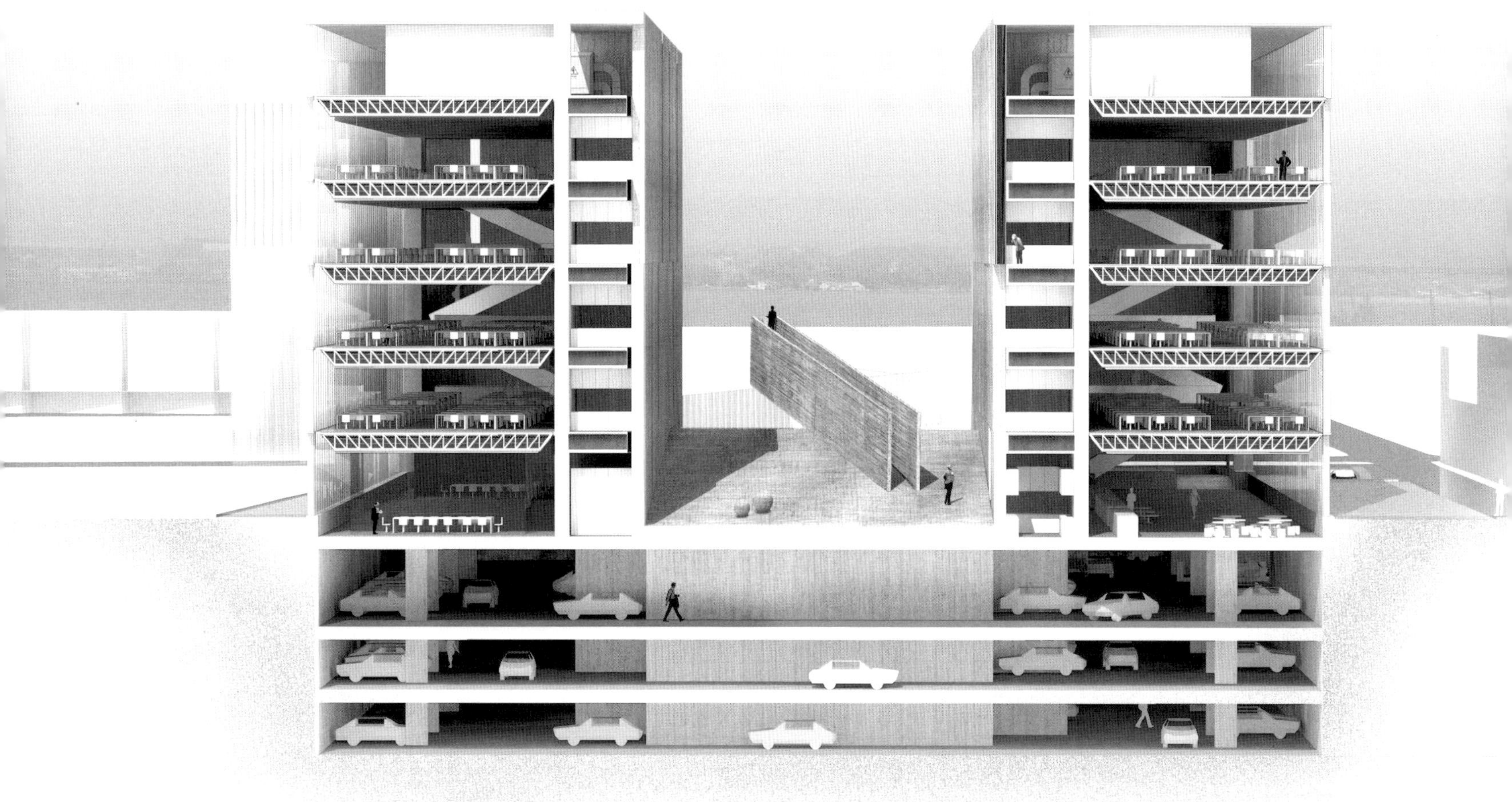

Open Source Creativity: Design as a Participatory Process

Interview with Alejandro Aravena by Michael Juul Holm

MJH: We talked quite extensively about the participatory processes in building specific types of social housing, and I thought maybe we could talk a little about creation and participatory processes as a broader phenomenon, and the open source philosophy applied to creation. Could you expand a bit on that? I know that you will be showing a project in the Louisiana exhibition about a chair and how that was created.

AA: Well, we have actually given a name to this approach so that we can explain to our clients what they're getting, or what we're going to do. We call it WE, Workshop Elemental. Whenever the *question* at the outset of the process is not clear, we suggest identifying the problem *together with the client*. When we first met the lamp and light-company Artemide in Milan about the design of two lamps, it was not clear if what they wanted from us was an object, a system, or merely technology. If we go to Buenos Aires – the bank building – in principle they wanted a house, but it was not clear where it was to be situated, what the agenda of the city was, nor the expectations of the people living around the building. Whenever you have a problem where the edges are blurred, we want to make sure first that we are all on the same page as regards the question, and only then jump to what could possibly be the answer. It was like: "Okay, in order to understand what the question is, let's meet there physically for a couple of days, morning, afternoon and evening, two or three days in a row." We normally ask the client to call any person they think may have specific issues, concerns, fears, expectations or potential benefits in their own field. Then we begin to approach the issue. For example with a security guy: a bank in Buenos Aires will have to deal with security, so let's have the department of security come and explain what type of codes they follow, how to measure a safe environment. If they need to get approval from an institution in the US, though they're building in Argentina, we want to know in advance. That kind of thing. We also include logistics employees from the bank – in case they need to provide catering for 200 people. How will that work? Or specific consultants who can foresee, even though they're not the client, that the people around the neighborhood may have expectations of this or that, or a specific problem. The neighbors are perhaps waiting for something to be done at last, so they would also like to benefit.

We begin from this pragmatic point of view. It is very important that we get quantifiable data, so all the things that you can measure, like the budget or the number of square meters, must be as clear as possible. But also the kind of practical and psychological matters that, unless we identify them very early on, could end up becoming a real problem. All this kind of information is part of the creative process, first of all in the sense of bringing the constraints, the expectations, the fears and the potentials of the project to the surface. And it has to be short. Normally, after we shut up and just listen, it is done within a couple of days – very quickly, we try to translate the input intuitively into a 'what if' kind of thing: What if we do this? And then we submit a proposal for the approval of all the people that came to inform us. We translate it very quickly in order to iterate it and make any mistakes at the very beginning. When we did social housing, the process started because we knew part of the project was physically going to be built by people themselves anyway, even if we would not have wanted it this way. And given that there was not enough money, and we would not be able to do everything, we wanted to know from the people what were their priorities.

— We talked about the water heater and the bathtub …

For example. But that evolved in a more general way, because in the case of a bank, there may not be a budget issue, but you still want to get the information 'between the lines' from them. What is an absolute must, and what, in the event we have to negotiate among all the forces at play, leaves scope for deviation from the original brief? So this approach has been applied so far to a lamp for a building, as in Buenos Aires. We listen to all the different stakeholders, and it's been surprising for us to see how our intuition works relatively quickly if we listen very proactively to the right people. When you think out loud together, people feel that they can follow the way you arrive at a conclusion. People are not presented with just: Okay, so here it is, you approve it or you don't. They understood the constraints, what the possibilities were. When you're cooking with somebody, I think a dish has a different taste depending on the people you cook with. Even though it was our task to translate all that into a proposal, we're not giving an absolute answer to the people, we're sharing the process.

— When you say intuition, you're actually talking about your professionalism and your skills: Something more than gut feeling. Intuition is a blend of skills, knowledge, talent, feeling, professionalism and experience …

I think sometimes we don't even know exactly what kind of design we need to produce. The first idea comes from intuition, and we go at it hard until it holds up – or doesn't, and we have to move over to something else. If we prefer the word intuition, it's because you might think that after building an equation and identifying its terms very clearly, whether they are highly concrete and measurable, or more intangible, like 'character' or 'mood' or fears and emotions, then in the end it's just a question of pressing 'enter', and you will get a solution, an answer. But in reality, it still requires that risk of jumping into the void. There's no direct cause-and-effect relationship between the premises of the question and the answer given. If there's any art in this trade, it may be in the capacity to jump from all the data you've collected into proposal mode, without having anything clear, at least not consciously. If you're fair to the information that you've collected, the jump into the proposal is a mysterious thing – you know, it's a mystery how it works. We just want it *not* to be a question of tastes. Intuition is a powerful tool that integrates more information than you think you have.

— Exactly. But something like the chair that you are presenting in this exhibition is much simpler, so it's different, right?

The chair actually starts from a very concrete personal need. I didn't have furniture in my house. I needed to have chairs to sit and eat with the children. Instead of going out to buy chairs for the dining room – you can't just buy *one,* you need to buy at least six, and you multiply the cost of the cheapest chair you can find that is at least some way decent; if it's beyond your budget, that's it. And I was already asking a carpenter to help with the shelves and a table. I wanted to approach the chair the same way: Can I design something that I can build myself? I go to the local Home Depot for something to take off the shelf, only sawn the length of the board, something to build that requires no skill – because I have no skill. And the result should not be something that you have to make a lot of excuses for, like, you know, "I'm not a good builder" or "I didn't have the money." The result shouldn't give away all your inadequacies. And the problem can be overcome with the right design – that was the assumption. It started out with: Okay, how many ways are there to make a knot, a three-dimensional knot, if you don't have carpentry skills? It's always flat on a corner, never on the longest side of the piece of wood. I think it's called a Cartesian knot or something, it has a name. I knew that the chair is maybe the most difficult design object, because it requires such great precision to understand the length, height and width as well as the resistance of the materials. You change things one or two centimeters and it's a completely different world – it's uncomfortable. So I began to work with the task myself, and came up with a combination of two materials. One is wood, something that is easily applied from any home improvement retailer. And the other one is felt, because we had a roll of felt, an incredible thing that we found many years ago in an old factory in Santiago. Pure black wool from Patagonia, one centimeter thick. It's an amazing product, but the owner wanted to get rid of it because he was selling all his stuff. So we said, okay, let's buy it, and we'll try to do something with it. But we didn't, we just stored it and it stayed there for years. Since it was available, I tried to combine the wood with this felt. And, again, so as not to have to call somebody who knows how to sew the material, we used only screws. And in the seventh or eighth version, it became something that was okay, because we had then come to a sort of understanding with the material, the stretching of the felt. It was comfortable to sit in, but not as a dinner chair – you have to eat sitting up rather straight. You kind of sank into the chair. So when the initial designing was done, we thought, well, it is so simple, I could even put it together myself, and it doesn't look as if you have to apologize for it. Maybe other people can build it as well? All the people that may have the same problem I had: Can we have a nice simple chair in a good quality, but very simply built?

We could have given the franchise to some small shop, but we thought: What about the jail? Somebody had told us that in the jail there was a carpentry workshop. Basically a program for teaching skills to inmates, so they have a bit of a profession, something to work with once they're out. As a former inmate, you have a record. If your record isn't clean, you don't get a job, and if you're not given a job when you get out of jail – then what do you do? The way the program works in the jail is that it is used with the prisoners with the worst behavior, the so-called 'baddest of the bad', to see if something can be done for the no-hopers. We went there just two weeks ago. It was the kind of thing you can't even imagine. It's an alternative planet, a parallel world. It was a very impressive experience. The jail is really crowded – actually, it has double the number of people it has capacity for. A room of 2x3 meters sleeps 12-18 people. One person dies each week in fights ...

— So can you work with this crowd?

That is our intention. These people want to do something that they can feel proud of. The situation is very complicated though. Among the 'baddest', you're not allowed to be good. So the moment they are offered this opportunity and go to the workshop, it's like betraying the code of being really bad. They may still have family outside. If the children, for example, or the spouse can say, well, he's not a killer or whatever, he's a carpenter – not a criminal but a carpenter – that completely changes the game for them. Here we have an object that is simple, but the simplicity of the operations doesn't alter the quality of the final product. Can we share this so that we all benefit? It will require some skills, but you don't have to be a master carpenter, you just need to be a *careful* carpenter. And if that produces a shared benefit, we may also achieve some scale in producing the thing for them.

This is what we call *Surdico*, as opposed to *Nordico*. In Spanish we call Nordic design *Diseño Nordico*. To us, Diseño Nordico is quality: simplicity and elegance. We see the history of Scandinavian or Nordic design as a moment when the means of production, particularly of furniture, went from handmade to machine-made. But at first that leap meant trying to ask the machine to do what the hand was doing, so there was a lot of, you know, 'decoration' that was done with machines to pretend they had as much value as the handmade thing. Then all of a sudden, somebody understood: The logic of the machine is different, so maybe our notion of *quality* also has to be transferred somewhere else? And design bridged the gap between the new means of production and the old standards of ethical-aesthetical approaches to making. So the equivalent of the machines at that time in Northern Europe is now, in the Southern hemisphere, non-skilled labor; a human footprint with a narrative that produces benefits within a longer chain. So that's the equivalent of our machines: Can we improve the human footprint of objects, so that if you trace the object back, you will learn who benefited from it, and you will prefer the one that has had more benefits. I guess we can't think of anyone needing it more than the 'baddest of the bad' in jail!

Even if you don't tell the story, when you look at the thing you should be able to like it instantly: "I'm going to buy it. It looks nice, it's a fair enough price. It has quality in its making, the materials and aesthetics are just fine." If you then trace it back, it turns out it has more layers, but it should be able to make a first impact as an artefact of quality. This is the approach we have called Surdico, and we thought: What better place to show this approach than at an epicenter of the Nordico design?

— Interesting. A lot of the quality, in my opinion, of Nordico design, classic Danish design, comes from the fact that at the time when they started industrializing production, there were still a number of very skilled craftsmen. All Danish designers of that time went to the craftsmen and asked how to do stuff, from crucial processes to tiny but important details. It becomes a real problem for design when there are no craftsmen of that kind, because you have no one to ask. Now there's a movement of young people going back to something that is handcrafted, trying to reopen the wells of the material wisdom of the old crafts because it's just clearly rewarding and very interesting for them.

The thing is, if I wanted to make my own clothes, for example, of course it would look awful and I would have to start explaining why it looks so shitty. Can we use design to fill that gap so it isn't so obvious, doesn't come to the surface? Design may play a role in creating a high quality result given simplicity of means. That may play a role in this notion of Surdico design. It's like starting from the brick and saying: I don't want to cut any bricks, so that restriction is the motive force. In this case, can I take something that doesn't require any other operation than straight cutting with a saw, at the store, not at home? If I have to do it myself, by hand, it will end up bad. Any piece has to have only four sides. If you have six sides, for example from taking out a corner, it becomes too complicated. I can't do that. Everything must be 90 degrees; that constraint keeps it simple and direct. The kids had an opinion about it, our secretary has an opinion about it, everyone has an opinion about it. Everybody in the office was talking about the chair, and it wasn't really participatory design, but for me the current state of the chair is a kind of 'open source product'. Because in the state it has right now, without any talent you can make something; but maybe the guys in jail ... there's a culture in jail of carving stuff. Normally it would be figures or sculptures of Christ or frames for pictures – you buy that stuff as philanthropy, not because you necessarily like it. But in this case the individual inmate can actually also add something to the design. It could be an element we don't even understand yet. Maybe it has to do with the pieces that give tension to the felt. Maybe there is room for improvement, maybe the joints can work without the screw, another piece of wood can be added – it's a really open source product. It is so simple. When you see the process, you immediately understand the way to re-do it and to expand on it.

ELEMENTAL

Silla

2018: A need for a new dining room chair in Alejandro Aravena's own home and the choise of using the principle at hand as well as rational straightforward design created the design of a new chair. Going about every task on the basis of Elemental's specific design philosophy – not necessarily based on specialized knowledge, but merely on common sense – made Aravena try making a chair in an ordinary material easily accessible to everyone. Using wood from an ordinary do-it-yourself centre and a roll of felt found at the studio, Aravena tried out the design of the chair through various tests. The prototype was passed on to a Chilean prison employing the prisoners in a carpentry as part of their preparations for life outside the prison. The fundamental idea is that a product does not have to carry a designer label, but can be shared with everyone as a kind of "open source" design which in turn can be improved by the next designer – which in this case would be the inmate carpenters in the prison. Elemental calls the design *Surdico* – taking inspiration from the simple and classical furniture design in Scandinavia (*Nordico*).

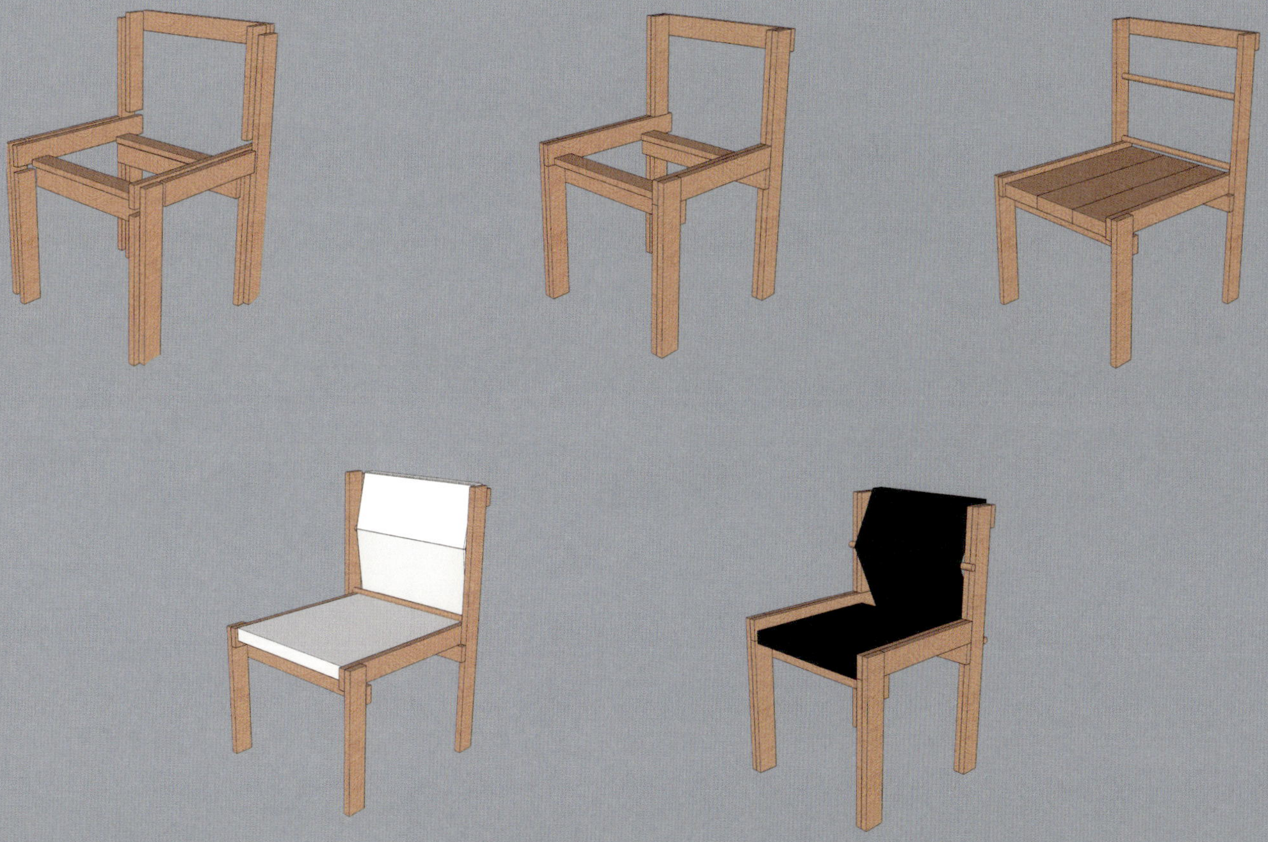

CAFÉ
VERDURAS
Sabores
Postres
JUMBO

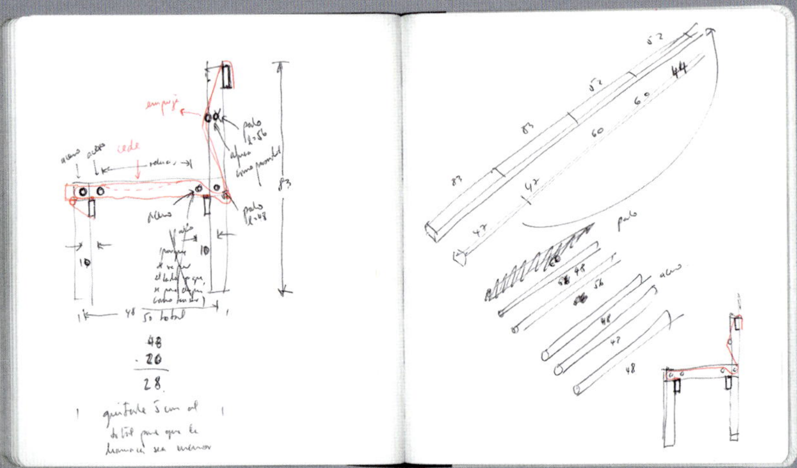

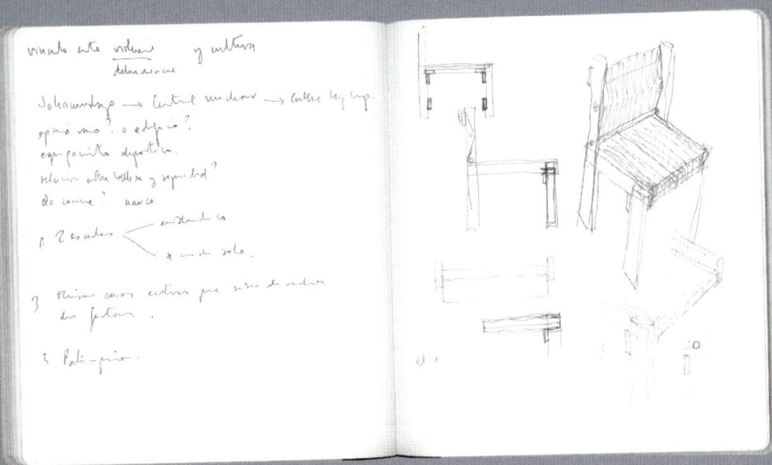

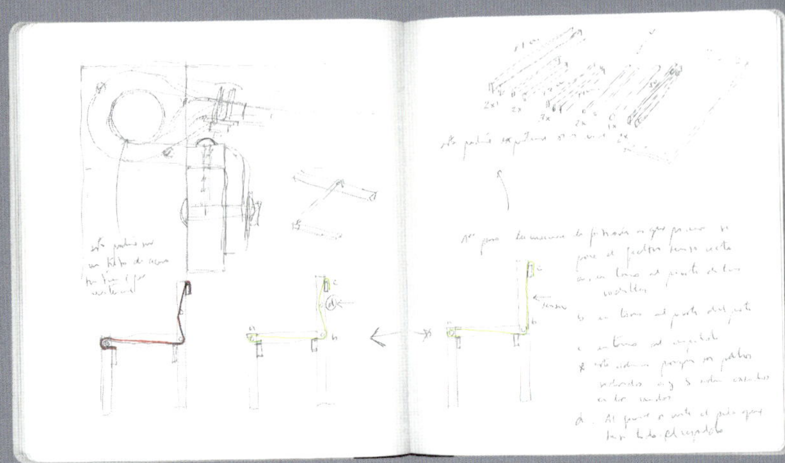

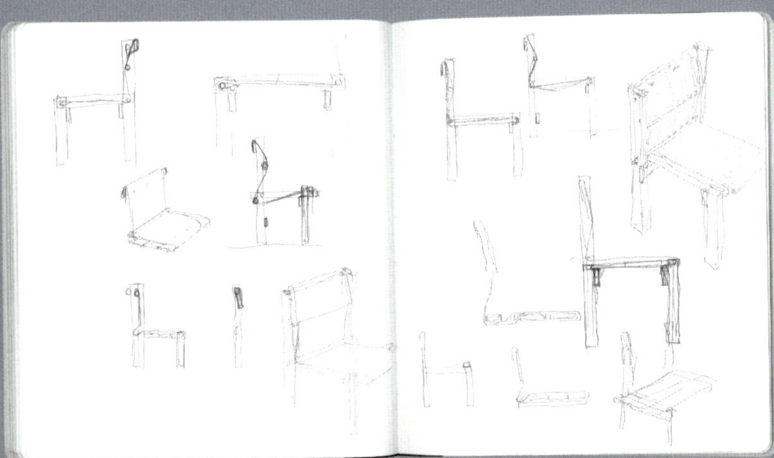

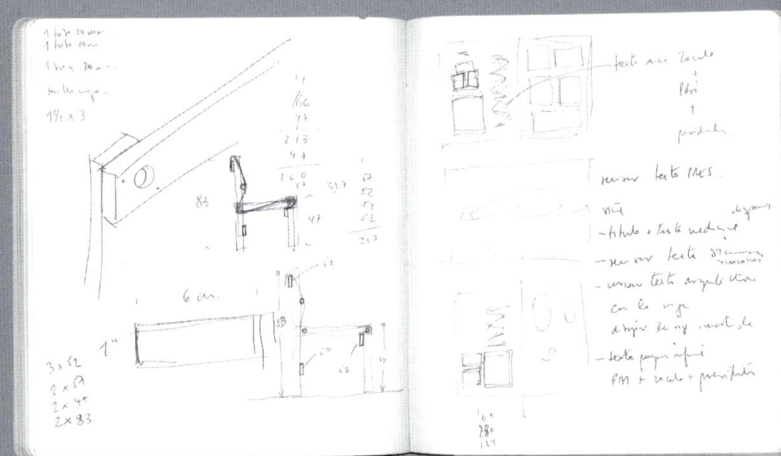

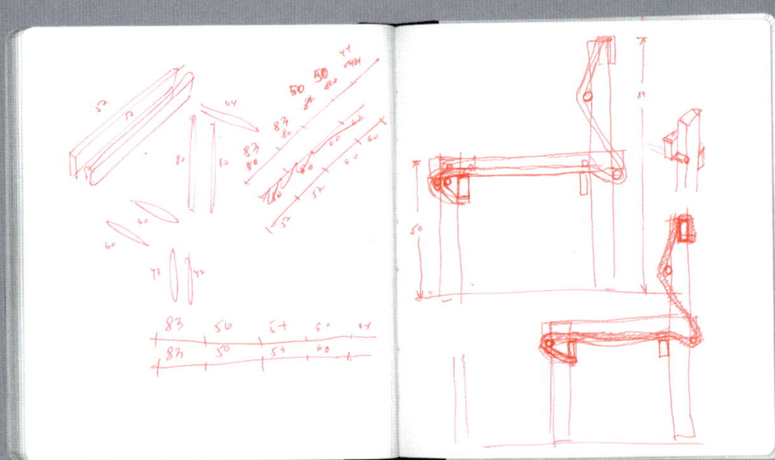

IDBG New Country Office Argentina

IDGB New Country Office Buenos Aires Argentina

The commission was to design the Inter-American Development Bank according to the city plan for Villa 31, the most prominent slum in Buenos Aires. 50,000 people live in this central area just across the train tracks that separate it from the most expensive neighbourhood. The area has issues with drug-dealing and safety, but is also a place where hardworking people looking for opportunities settle in the city. The bank was a major opportunity to bring quality services to the neighbourhood, but the neighbourhood also had the potential to bring the bank closer to the ultimate purpose of its operations. With 500 metres to the closest public transport, pedestrian and vehicle accessibility were a challenge in terms of security for the bank's staff and clients. Recommending building the bank elsewhere was unfeasible, so Elemental proposed a building, bridge and park in one in a project that created connectivity via a footbridge linking two very different parts of the city. The terms of the proposal were set by a new highway plan, raising the project to a height of 18 metres. Elemental designed 'a transparent bar', which at night is transformed into an urban lamp that improves security here and for the neighbourhood, as well as creating a landmark in the urban landscape.

IDGB New Country Office Argentina
Design Period: 2018-2019
Building Area: 3,800 m² officies +
6,000 m² green areas and public space

The location of the building made it possible for Elemental to address the bank's security issues, at the same time as providing views and plenty of daylight and natural ventilation.

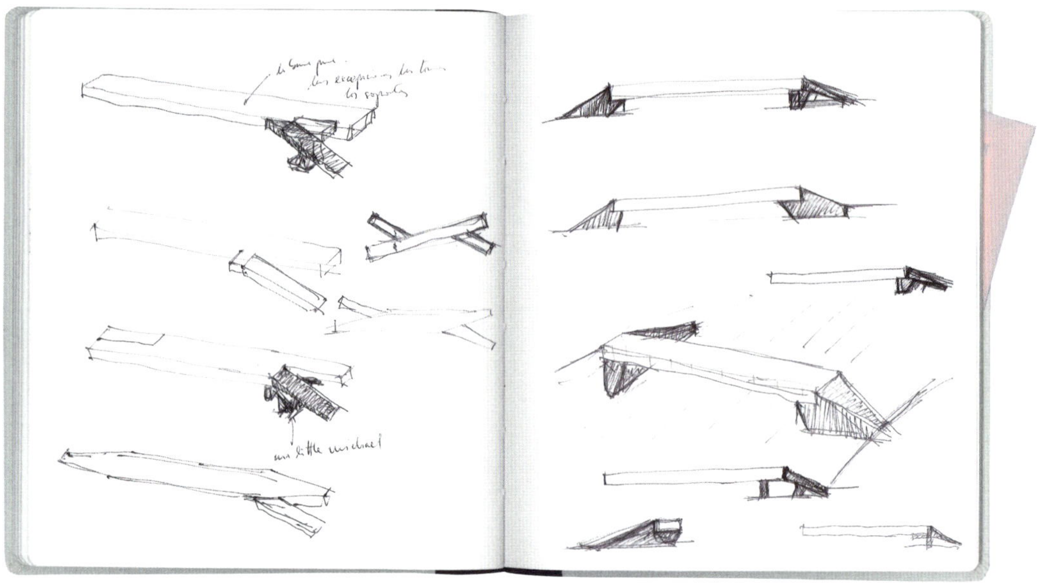

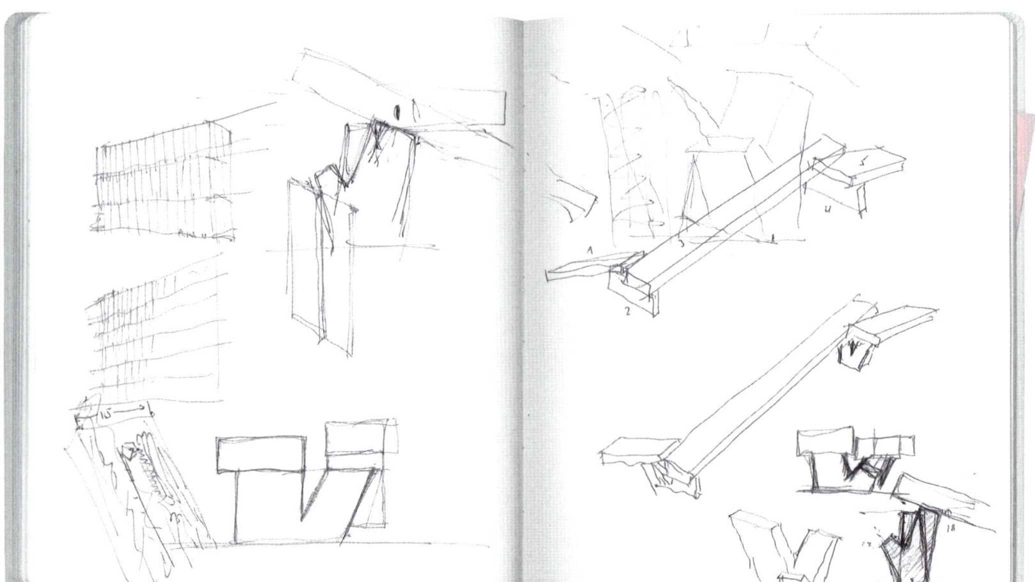

The footbridge connecting two parts of Buenos Aires previously separated by a 'river' of train traffic that made it difficult for people to get from one part of the city to the other

Saint Edwards University Dormitories Austin, Texas, USA

The residence should include a 300 rooms dormitory, a dining hall, classrooms and a chapel. Elemental compares the residence to a monastery where the monks' cells all relate to a dining hall, a library and a chapel: a suite of repetitive units is organized around larger important assembly points. The building consists of a plinth gathering all the public functions on top of which the private rooms are placed. Like many of Elemental's other buildings, the point of departure is a solid building element which is excavated and adapted to fit the various functions of the building. Lastly the shape of the building is adjusted so that niches is created providing as many rooms as possible with a view and a natural inflow of light. To give protection from the hot and dry climate, the external walls of the building are rough in contrast to the soft expression of the interior glass surfaces. The cavities and cracks that are the results of the excavation of the monolithic block create cool and ventilated outdoor spaces, inspired by the Hamilton Pool cave, which is the only naturally cool outdoor space in the surrounding area. As per request by the contractor reference is made to the red pitched roofs of the old main building of the university. The red colour scale is repeated on the inner side of the building between the glass panels.

Saint Edwards University Dormitories
Design/Construction Period: 2006-2008
Building Area: 30,000 m² (12,000 m² dorms + 18,000 m² parking)

Like the model, this sketch shows how the building has been created by carving hollows out of a solid block. This approach to a monolith creates a natural flow between multiple, singular building forms.

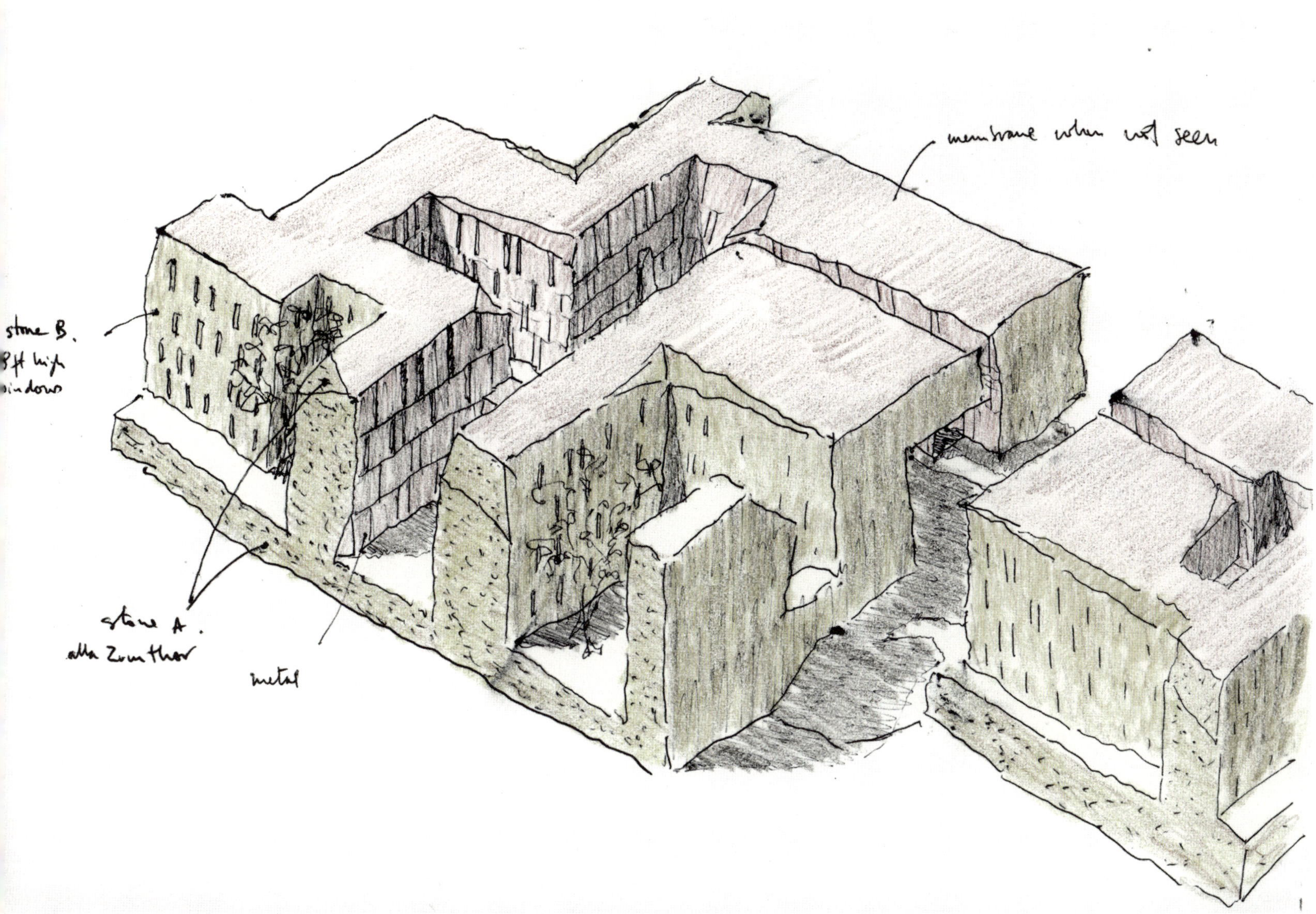

Even though the geometry is rectangular, the outdoor areas are reminiscent of the natural caves and ravines of rocky landscapes.

Santiago Astronomy Space

2014-2015: In 2020, 70% of the capacity of astronomical observation in the world will be concentrated in Chile. There is no other human activity or grouping of natural resources with this level of concentration. In order to take advantage of this unique feature, the proposal was put forth to build the Astronomical Observatory of Santiago on the summit of Cerro San Cristóbal, a site that will allow the citizens to become more familiar with the knowledge that revolves around this science and which explains why Chile has become so important in this field. The Elemental project intends to integrate the historical monument Observatory UC Foster and will enable, in real time, sharing the view offered by all the other large telescopes of North Chile.

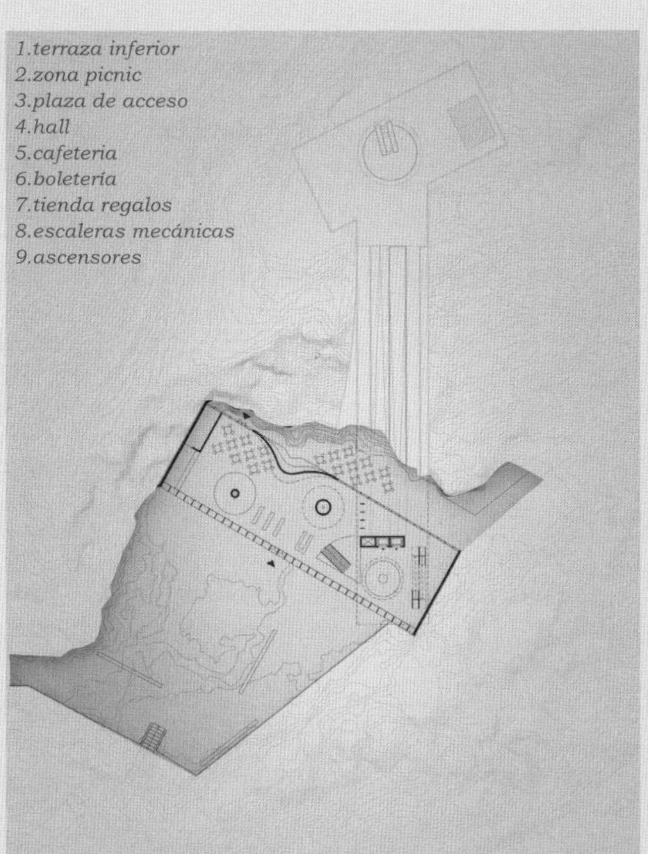

Nivel Acceso | Cafeteria | Tienda Regalos

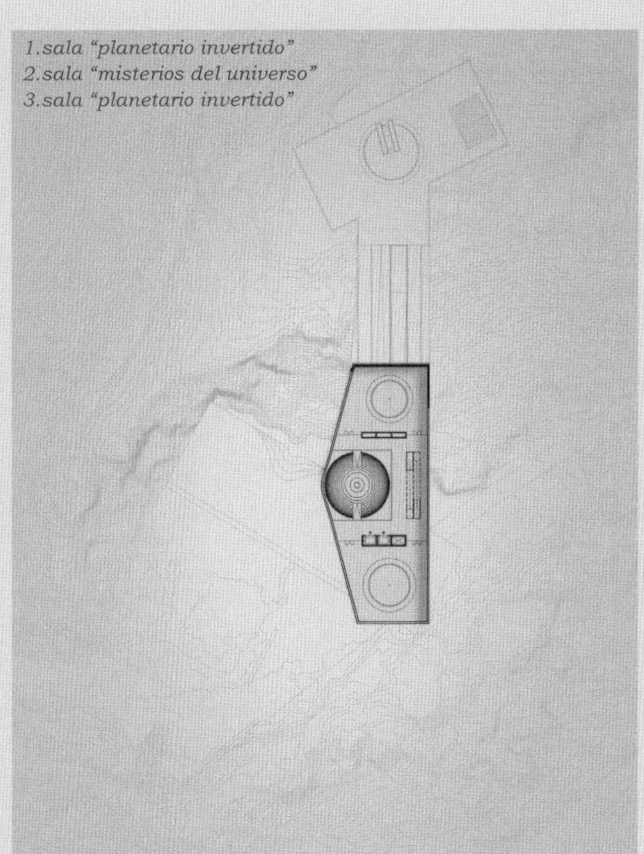

Nivel 2 - 3 - 4 | Salas de Exhibiciones

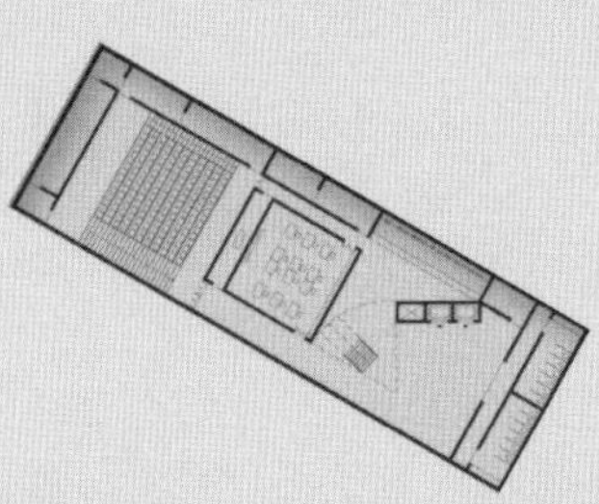

Nivel -1 - Centro Convensiones

1.auditorio 200 personas
2.sala mutliuso
3.baños públicos
4.hall exposición temporaria
5.bodega / salas técnicas
6.guardaropa

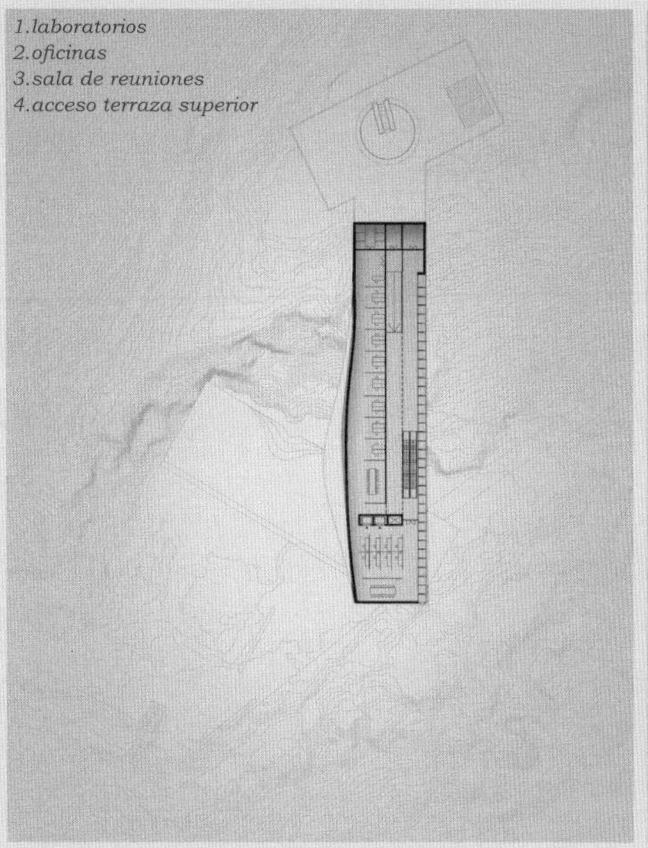

Nivel 5 | Oficinas y LaboratoriosSalas de Exhibiciones

Nivel Cubierta | Observatorio Foster-UC y Mirador

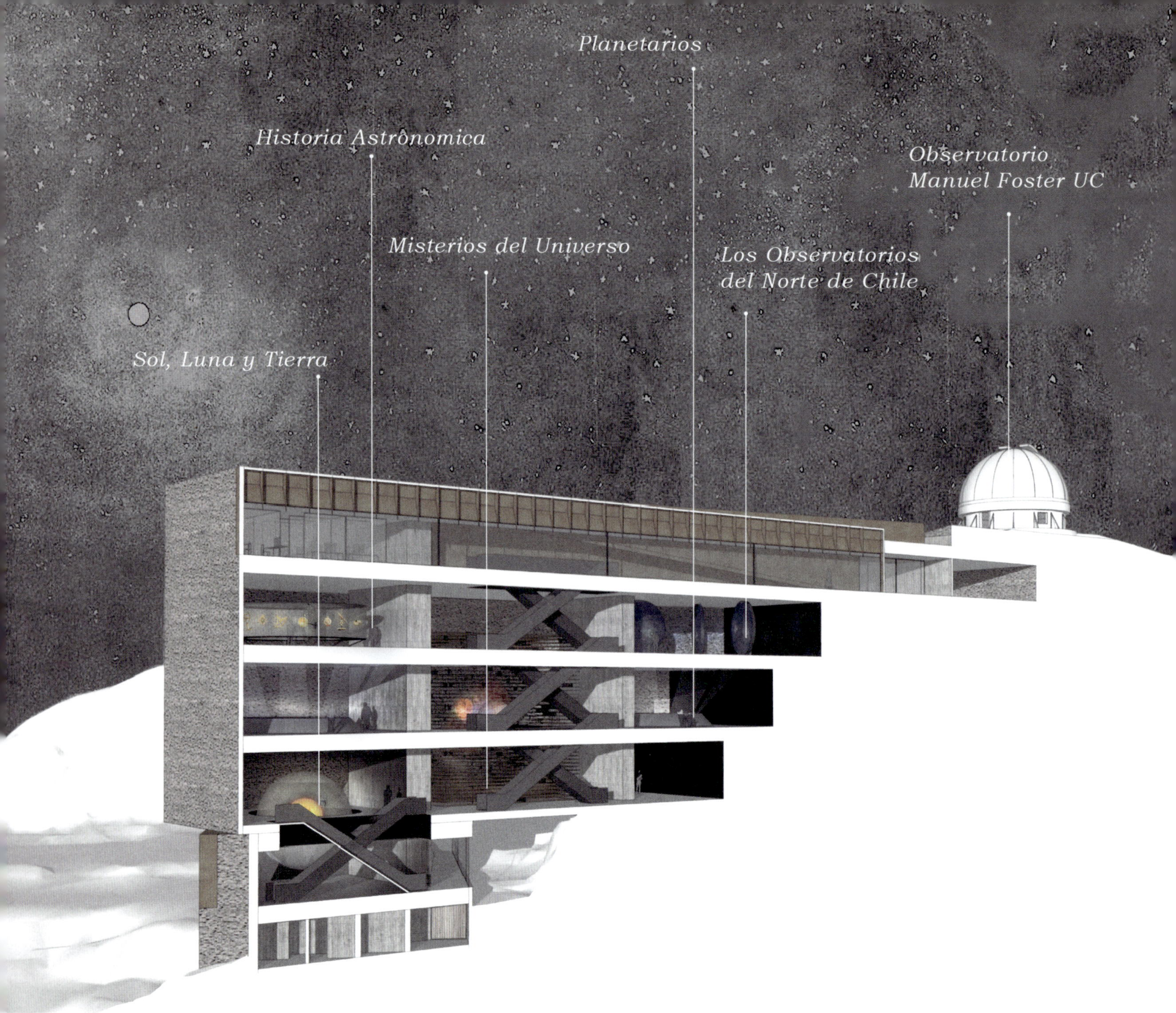

Planetarios
Historia Astrònomica
Observatorio
Manuel Foster UC
Misterios del Universo
Los Observatorios
del Norte de Chile
Sol, Luna y Tierra

The interior including among others a planetarium in which the audience can feel the emptiness of the universe, a holographic representation of the solar system and live broadcasts of what the great telescopes of the north of the country are observing in real time.

The Architect's Studio

ELEMENTAL
Alejandro Aravena

Edited by Mette Marie Kallehauge and Lærke Rydal Jørgensen

Graphic Design: Søren Damstedt and Camilla Jørgensen, Trefold
Translation from the Danish: Jane Rowley (Far from Elementary and project descriptions) and Glen Garner (Foreword)
Proofreading: James Manley
Front Cover: UC Innovation Center Anacleto Angelini. Photo: Felipe Diaz

Litho: Narayana Press
Print: Narayana Press
ISBN Lars Müller Publishers: 978-3-03778-572-0
ISBN Louisiana Museum of Modern Art: 978-87-93659-10-0
Printed in Denmark 2018

Lars Müller Publishers is supported by the Swiss Federal Office of Culture with a structural contribution for the years 2016–2020.

Lars Müller Publishers
Zürich, Switzerland
www.lars-mueller-publishers.com

Louisiana Museum of Modern Art
Humlebæk, Denmark
www.louisiana.dk

Distributed in North America by ARTBOOK | D.A.P.
www.artbook.com

This catalogue is published on the occasion of the exhibition
The Architect's Studio
So Far ... ELEMENTAL | Alejandro Aravena
Louisiana Museum of Modern Art
10 October 2018 – 28 February 2019

Curator: Kjeld Kjeldsen
Co-Curator: Mette Marie Kallehauge
Curatorial Coordinator/Registrar: Marianne Ahrensberg
Exhibition Producer and Conservator: Ulrik Staal Strange Dinesen
Exhibition Architect: Brian Lottenburger
Graphic Designer: Marie d'Origny Lübecker

www.louisiana.dk

The exhibition is supported by

Realdania

Sponsor of Louisiana's architectural exhibitions

Louisiana's Main Corporate Partners

NØRGAARD PAA STRØGET

REPUBLIC OF Fritz Hansen®

UBS

Supports programs and exhibitions at Louisiana Museum of Modern Art